Praise for *Resonate*

"Nancy Duarte boils down great presentations to the essence of what connects people—great stories. As a leader, you need to connect, convince, and change people with your words—so don't you dare start your next presentation without consulting this book first!"

Charlene Li
Author, Open Leadership
Founder, Altimeter Group

"Storytelling, empathy, and creativity are fundamental to the way we communicate, learn, and grow. *Resonate* teaches us how to access and master these gifts in meaningful and productive ways."

Biz Stone
Twitter Co-Founder

"*Resonate* takes you on a beautiful journey illustrating how to construct and deliver the kind of presentations that are truly remarkable, memorable...and may even change the world. Anyone with ambition to make a difference in this world needs to get this important book. Nancy has made another remarkable contribution!"

Garr Reynolds
Author of *Presentation Zen* and *The Naked Presenter*

"TED knows first-hand how ideas that spread change the world. If you read *Resonate,* you'll learn how to present ideas that stand out, are repeated, and create change."

Tom Rielly
Community Director, TED Conferences

"Nancy knows a secret, and she's not shy about sharing it: If you are intentional about your presentations, if you tell a story on purpose, if you set out to cause the change you say you want, you'll succeed. This book goes a long way in selling you on making that choice."

Seth Godin
Speaker, Blogger, and Author

"There is a stark difference between facts and a story, between an image and a design, between conveying information and moving people. These differences distinguish people who yell but aren't heard from those whose whispers resonate loudly and clearly. This is a gorgeous book. Powerful ideas, visually delectable, and with life-changing insight."

Jennifer Aaker
General Atlantic Professor of Marketing
at Stanford Graduate School of Business
and Co-Author of *The Dragonfly Effect*

"At the heart of leadership and learning is great storytelling. *Resonate* will both inspire and give you the tools to teach, motivate, and encourage audiences not just to listen but to change and to act...and the world needs a lot more of that! This book is a keeper, one to be read and reread by anyone in the business of persuasion."

Jacqueline Novogratz
CEO of Acumen Fund
and Author of *The Blue Sweater*

resonate

PRESENT VISUAL
STORIES THAT
TRANSFORM
AUDIENCES

resonate

PRESENT VISUAL
STORIES THAT
TRANSFORM
AUDIENCES

Nancy Duarte
author of *slide:ology*

WILEY

John Wiley & Sons, Inc.

Resonate

Present Visual Stories that Transform Audiences
by Nancy Duarte

This book is printed on acid-free paper. ⊚

Copyright © 2010 by Nancy Duarte. All rights reserved.

Design and production by Duarte Design, Inc.

Published by John Wiley & Sons, Inc., Hoboken, New Jersey.
Published simultaneously in Canada.

For general information on our other products and services or for technical support, please
contact our Customer Care Department within the United States at (800) 762-2974, outside
the United States at (317) 572-3993 or fax (317) 572-4002.

Wiley also publishes its books in a variety of electronic formats. Some content that appears
in print may not be available in electronic books. For more information about Wiley products,
visit our web site at www.wiley.com.

ISBN: 978-0-470-63201-7

Printed in the United States of America

10 9 8 7 6 5

I miss you Daddy.

"The mystery lies in the use of language to express human life."

Eudora Welty

Acknowledgments

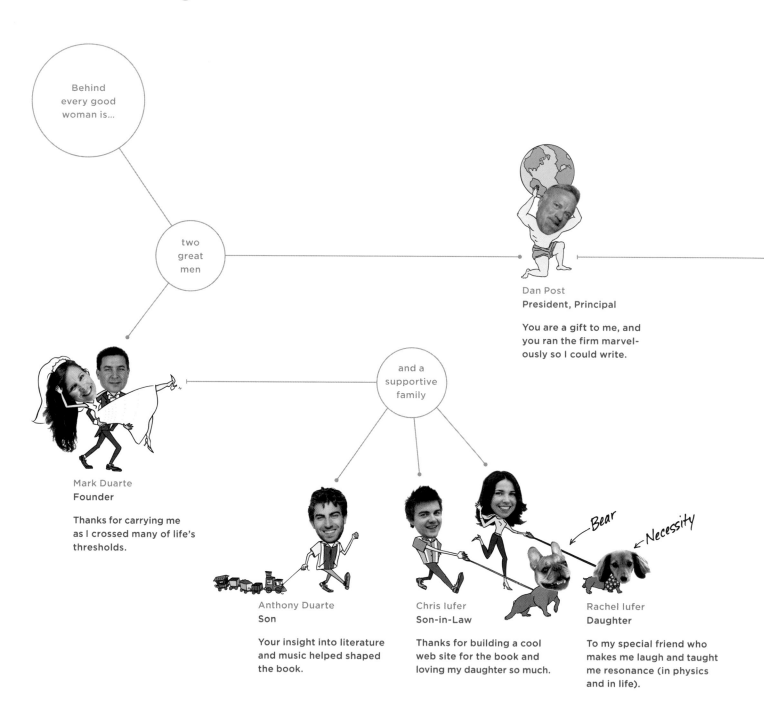

Behind every good woman is...

two great men

and a supportive family

Dan Post
President, Principal

You are a gift to me, and you ran the firm marvelously so I could write.

Mark Duarte
Founder

Thanks for carrying me as I crossed many of life's thresholds.

Anthony Duarte
Son

Your insight into literature and music helped shaped the book.

Chris Iufer
Son-in-Law

Thanks for building a cool web site for the book and loving my daughter so much.

Rachel Iufer
Daughter

To my special friend who makes me laugh and taught me resonance (in physics and in life).

←Bear

←Necessity

DUARTE

What a group of smart and inspired communicators. It's an honor to work with all of you.

Adam	James B.	Melissa
Alex	James N.	Michael
Anne	Jasper	Michal
April	Jessica	Michele
Brent	Jill	Nicole
Brooke	Jo	Oscar
Bruce	Jon	Paul
Carol	Jonathan	Paula
Chris F.	Josiah	Rob
Dan G.	Katie	Robin
Daniel	Kerry	Ryan F.
Darlene	Kevin	Ryan O.
Dave	Kyle	Stephanie
Doug	Laura	Steve
Drew	Liz	Terri
Ed	Lyndsey	Tricia
Elizabeth	M	Trish
Erik	Marisa	Vonn
Fabian	Mark H.	Yvette
Harris	Megan	
Helen	Melinda	

and a very talented team

Krystin Brazie
Ex Comm Manager

I never dreamed someone could take on so much of my load! Thanks.

Diandra Macias
Creative Director

The book is breathtaking, Diandra. Thank you for the hard work and years of friendship.

Michaela Kastlova
Designer

Thanks, Michaela, for being meticulous with the design.

Eric Albertson
Director of Instructional Design

You had the guts to murder my darlings and make me start over... and over...

Contents

Foreword

Great presentations are like magic. They amaze their audiences. And great presenters are like magicians. In addition to practicing regularly, both are reluctant to reveal the methods behind their performances. Among magicians, it is acceptable to reveal secrets to those who are committed to learning the art and becoming serious magicians. In that same context, Nancy Duarte is offering a one-of-a-kind learning opportunity, available to those who take presentations seriously.

Resonate cracks the code on how to orchestrate the invisible attributes that shape transformative audience experiences.

It all starts with becoming a better storyteller. Possessing the power to influence the beliefs of others and create acceptance of new ideas is timeless. The value of storytelling transcends language and culture. As we move rapidly toward a future of improved connections between people, cross-pollinated creativity, and digital effects, stories still represent the most compelling platform we have for managing our imaginations—and our infinite data. More than any other form of communication, the art of telling stories is an integral part of the human experience. Those who master it are often afforded great influence and enduring legacy.

Nancy Duarte understands how to align ideas to create world-shaping responses. No one else has been so exclusively focused on mastering the presentation space as a discipline, and few have worked across a broader spectrum of client profiles and communication challenges. She is passionate about building systems that make creative results replicable and scalable.

Nancy Duarte has an insatiable curiosity about processes—with a relentless drive to codify practices that have defied specification by others.

Over two decades and dozens of economic cycles, she has attracted extraordinary talent to her organization, and with a singular vision has established it as the industry leader. In fact, Duarte Design now lays claim to working with half of the world's top fifty brands, and many of its most innovative thinkers. The analysis and insights in this book are distinctly competent.

Knowing a magic secret doesn't make you a magician. You have to do more than just read instructions. Without exception, great presenters are very deliberate about learning how to refine and reveal their ideas. They hone their words, sweat the structure, and practice their craft rigorously. They constantly seek and adapt to feedback.

If great presentations were easy to build and deliver, they wouldn't be such an extraordinary form of communication. *Resonate* is intended for people with ambition, purpose, and an uncommon work ethic.

Applied with passion and purpose, the concepts in this book will accelerate your career trajectory or propel your social cause. At Duarte Design, we see it happen every day. Few pursuits in professional self-improvement have as much potential leverage. All you really need is an idea. Most of the influential presenters throughout history—including those profiled in this book—started with one really good idea. You may be incubating that class of idea, or you may be one slide deck away from it; either way, you need to get it out in the open so that we can all benefit from it.

Nancy Duarte wants you to become a thought leader. She hopes you can give the rest of us the structure and direction we need to navigate challenges and opportunities, and help us interpret our goals. She expects you to make sense of chaos. She dares you to be transparent and evocative, motivational and persuasive. Above all, she trusts you to inspire action for our greater good.

Dan Post
President and Principal, Duarte Design

Enjoy the journey!

Introduction

Language and power are inextricably linked. The spoken word pushes ideas out of someone's head and into the open so humankind can contend with adopting or rejecting its validity. Moving an idea from its inception to adoption is hard, but it's a battle that can be won simply by wielding a great presentation.

Presentations are a powerfully persuasive tool, and when packaged in a story framework, your ideas become downright unstoppable. Story structures have been employed for hundreds of generations to persuade and delight every known culture.

Two years ago, I set out to uncover how story applies to presentations. There seemed to be a storylike magic to the presentations that caused change and spread broadly. Since I already had the context of thousands of presentations my firm had created for smart companies and causes, I studied what I didn't know: screenwriting, literature, mythology, and philosophy—allowing myself to be led on a fascinating journey.

Early in my research, I stumbled on this graphic made in 1863 by German dramatist Gustav Freytag that he used to visualize the five-act structure popular in Greek and Shakespearean dramas. It shows the "shape" of a dramatic story. The drama builds toward a climax and then resolves.

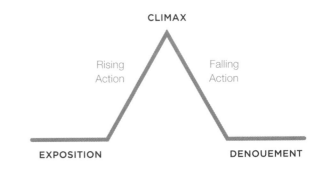

When I saw Freytag's pyramid, I knew that powerful presentations must also have a contour. I just didn't quite know what the shape looked like yet. I also knew that presentations are different from dramatic stories because in a presentation, it's rare to have a lone protagonist whose story builds toward a single climactic moment. Presentations have more layers and have disparate pieces of information to convey. Dramatic stories have a single climax as the crowning event whereas great presentations move along with multiple peaks that propel them forward.

I'll never forget the Saturday morning when I finally sketched out a shape. I knew that if it was accurate, I should be able to overlay it onto two very different yet game-changing presentations. So I painstakingly analyzed Steve Jobs's 2007 iPhone launch and Martin Luther King Jr.'s "I Have a Dream" speech. Both mapped to the form I had sketched. I cried. Literally. It felt like such a mystery had been revealed.

There's something sacred about stories. They have an almost supernatural power that should be wielded wisely. Religious scholars, psychologists, and mythologists have studied stories for decades to determine the secret to their power.

It's still the dawn of the information age, and we are all overwhelmed with too many messages bombarding us and trying to lure us to acquire and consume information (then repeat the process over and over). We are in a more selfish and cynical age, which makes it tempting to be detached. Technology has given us many ways to communicate, but only one is truly human: in-person presentations. Genuine connections create change.

You'll notice that *change* is a theme throughout the book. Most presentations are delivered to persuade people to change. All presentations have a component of persuasion to them. This notion may ruffle some feathers. But isn't there usually a desired outcome from what's classified as an informative presentation? Yes. You're moving your audience from being uninformed to being informed. From being uninterested in your subject to being interested. From being stuck in a process to being unstuck. Many times the audience needs to do something with the information you're conveying, which makes your presentation persuasive.

So whether you're an engineer, teacher, scientist, executive, manager, politician, or student, presentations will play a role in shaping your future. The future isn't just a place you'll go; it's a place you will invent. Your ability to shape your future depends on how well you communicate where you want to be when you get there.

How to Use *Resonate*

Resonate is a prequel to my first book, *Slide:ology.* When I wrote *Slide:ology,* I thought the most pressing need in communications was for people to learn how to visually display their brilliant ideas so they were clearer and less overwhelming for the audience to process. Come to find out, there was a much deeper problem. Gussying up slides that have meaningless content is like putting lipstick on a pig.

Presentations are broken systemically, and the methodology in *Resonate* uses story frameworks to create presentations that will engage, transform, and activate audiences. After more than twenty years of developing presentations for the best brands and thought leaders in the world, we've codified our Visual Story™ methodology so you can change your world!

Below are design elements to be aware of:

- The green www symbol signifies there's additional material at www.duarte.com about the subject.

- The Presentation Form™ is used as an analysis tool throughout the book and is visually expressed as a *sparkline* (a term developed by Edward Tufte).

- The **bold text** is for the reader who wants to just skim and get a nugget from each spread.

- The blue body text signifies my personal stories or excerpts from speeches.

- There are citations from several sources in the body copy, but some deserved extra emphasis and are pulled out in **orange text**.

This book is simultaneously an explanation, a how-to guide, and a business justification for story-based messaging. It will take you on a journey to a level of presentation literacy that very few have mastered. Using techniques from story and cinema, you will understand key steps for connecting to the audience, deferring to them as the hero, and creating a presentation that resonates.

Invest Your Time

Be forewarned: A high-quality in-person presentation takes time and planning, yet pressure on our time prevents us from preparing high-quality communications. It takes discipline to be a great communicator—it's a skill that will bring a big payoff to you personally and to your organization.

But a recent survey conducted by Distinction had some startling findings. Of the executives surveyed, over 86 percent said that communicating clearly impacts their careers and incomes yet only 25 percent put more than two hours into preparing for *very high-stakes* presentations. That's a big gap.

The result of investing in an important presentation is unparalleled in any other medium. When an idea is communicated effectively, people follow and change. Words that are carefully framed and spoken are the most powerful means of communication there is. The lifework of the communicators featured in this book are proof.

Hope you enjoy,

Nancy

DISTINCTION COMMUNICATION EXECUTIVE SURVEY RESULTS

1	2	3
How would you rank the importance of personal presentation skills in what you do?	What do you find the most challenging part of creating a presentation?	How much time do you spend practicing for a "high-stakes" presentation?
86.1% Communicating with clarity directly impacts my career and income.	**35.7%** Putting together a good message.	**12.1%** I seldom have time to practice at all.
13.8% I present from time to time but the stakes don't seem all that high.	**8.9%** Creating quality slides.	**16.2%** 5–30 minutes.
0% I don't do any formal presentations.	**13.8%** Delivering the presentation with confident skills.	**17.0%** 30 minutes to one hour.
	41.1% All of the above!	**29.2%** One to two hours.
		25.2% More than two hours!

©www.distinction-services.com

CHAPTER 1

Why Resonate?

Persuasion Is Powerful

Movements are started, products are purchased, philosophies are adopted, subject matter is mastered—all with the help of presentations.

Great presenters transform audiences. Truly great communicators make it look easy as they lure audiences to adopt their ideas and take action. This isn't something that just happens automatically; it comes at the price of long and thoughtful hours spent constructing messages that resonate deeply and elicit empathy.

Throughout the book, you'll learn from some of the greatest communicators. Each is different and yields a unique insight, yet they share a common thread: They all create a groundswell of support for their ideas. These communicators don't have to force or command their audiences to adopt their ideas. Instead, the audience responds willingly with a surge of support.

Great Communicators

MOTIVATOR
**Benjamin Zander,
Conductor, Boston
Philharmonic Orchestra**

MARKETER
**Beth Comstock,
Chief Marketing
Officer, GE**

POLITICIAN
**Ronald Reagan,
Former President of
the United States**

CONDUCTOR
**Leonard Bernstein,
Conductor, New York
Philharmonic Orchestra**

LECTURER
Richard Feynman,
Professor, California
Institute of Technology

PREACHER
John Ortberg,
Pastor, Menlo Park
Presbyterian Church

EXECUTIVE
Steve Jobs,
Chief Executive
Officer, Apple Inc.

ACTIVIST
Martin Luther King Jr.,
Civil Rights Activist

ARTIST
Martha Graham,
Contemporary Dancer

Resonance Causes Change

Presentations are most commonly delivered to persuade an audience to change their minds or behavior. Presenting ideas can either evoke puzzled stares or frenzied enthusiasm, which is determined by how well the message is delivered and how well it resonates with the audience. After a successful presentation, you might hear people say, "Wow, what she said really resonated with me."

But what does it mean to truly resonate with someone?

Let's look at a simple phenomenon in physics. If you know an object's natural rate of vibration, you can make it vibrate without touching it. **Resonance occurs when an object's natural vibration frequency responds to an external stimulus of the same frequency.** To the right is a beautiful visualization of resonance. My son poured salt onto a metal plate that he then hooked up to an amplifier so that the sound waves traveled through the plate. As the frequency was raised, the sound waves tightened and the grains of salt jiggled, popped, and then moved to a new place, organizing themselves into beautiful patterns as though they *knew* where they "belonged." www

There is more at www.duarte.com

How many times have you wished that students, employees, investors, or customers would snap, crackle, and pop to exactly where they need to be to create a new future?

It would be great if audiences were as compliant and unified in thought and purpose as these grains of salt. And they can be. **If you adjust to the frequency of your audience so that the message resonates deeply, they, too, will display self-organizing behavior.** Your listeners will see the place where they are to move to create something collectively beautiful. A groundswell.

The audience does not need to tune themselves to you—you need to tune your message to them. Skilled presenting requires you to understand their hearts and minds and create a message to resonate with what's already there. Your audience will be significantly moved if you send a message that is tuned to their needs and desires. They might even quiver with enthusiasm and act in concert to create beautiful results.

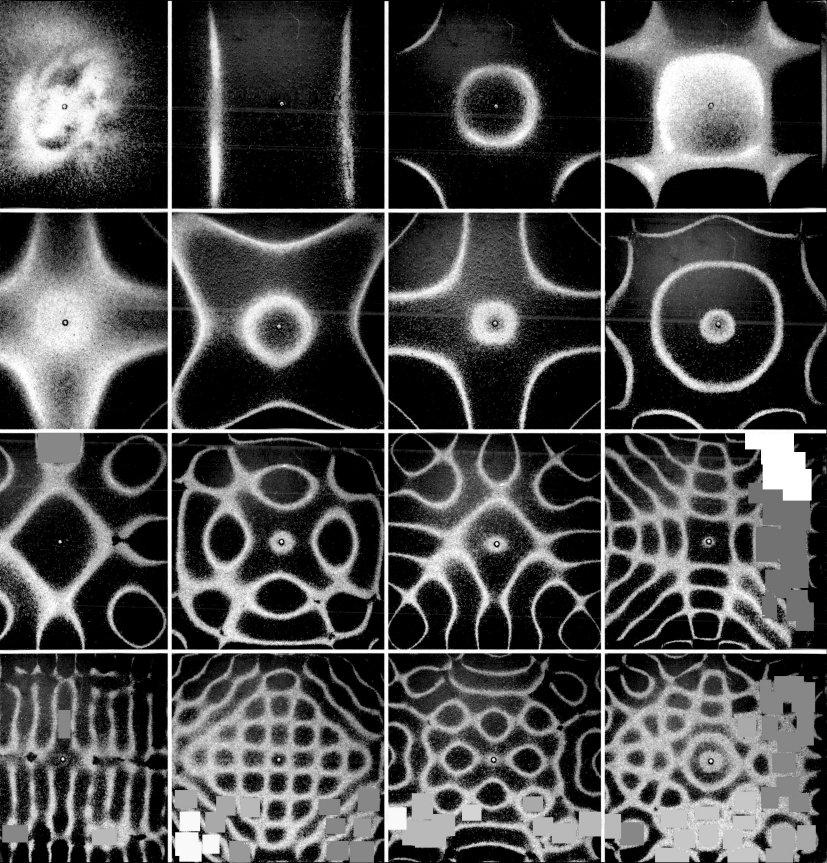

Change Is Healthy

Presentations are about change. Businesses, and indeed all professions, have to change and adapt in order to stay alive.

Organizations go through a life cycle of starting up, growing, maturing, and eventually declining—that is, unless they reinvent themselves. A business is usually founded because someone came up with a clear vision of the world in the future as an improved place. But that improved world quickly becomes an ordinary world. Once an organization arrives at maturity, it can't get too comfortable. To avoid potential decline, it must alter and adapt its strategy so it's at the right place at the right time in the future. If an organization doesn't take a new path, it will eventually wither. Communicating each move carefully to all stakeholders and clients becomes critical.

It takes gutsy intuitive skills to move toward an unknown future that involves unfamiliar risks and rewards, yet businesses must make these moves to survive. Companies that learn to thrive in the chronic flux and tension between *what is* and *what could be*

are healthier than those that don't. Many times the future cannot be quantified with statistics, facts, or proofs. Sometimes leaders have to let their gut lead them into uncharted territories where statistics haven't yet been generated.

An organization should make continual shifts and improvements to stay healthy. That makes even simple presentations at staff meetings a platform for persuasion. You need to persuade your team to self-organize at a distinct place in the future or it could bring the demise of the organization.

Getting ahead of the next curve requires courage and communication: Courage to determine the next bold move, and communication to keep the troops committed to the value of moving forward.

Rallying stakeholders to move together in a common course of action is all part of the innovation and survival process. Leaders at every level in an organization need to be skillful at creating resonance if that organization is to control its own destiny.

Business Transformation

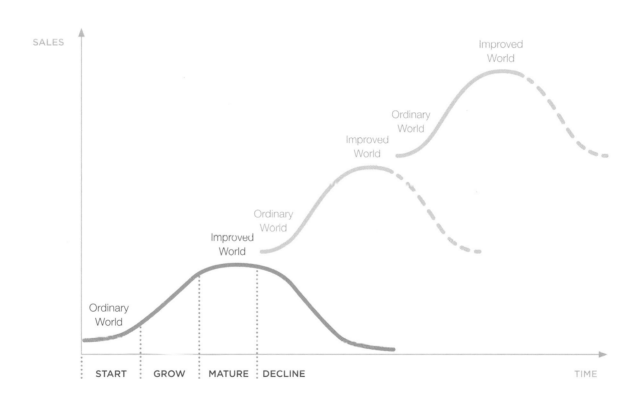

"Progress is impossible without change;
and those who cannot change their minds
cannot change anything."

George Bernard Shaw

Presentations Are Boring

Presentations are the currency of business activity because they are the most effective tool to transform an audience, yet many presentations are boring. Most are a dreadful failure of communication, and the rest are simply not interesting. Could there be a way to resuscitate them to a point where they not only show signs of life but actually engage audiences with rapt attention?

If you've been trapped in a bad presentation, you recognize the feeling almost immediately. You can tell within minutes that it's just not good; it doesn't take long to recognize a corpse! To make matters worse, it's becoming more and more difficult to keep an audience's attention as global cultures become media-rich environments. Slick ad agencies and Hollywood producers spend enormous amounts of time and money to build a pulse and rhythm into their media. While entertainment has raised the bar for audience engagement, presentations have become less engaging than ever.

So why then, if presentations are so bad, are they scheduled? People inherently know that connecting in person can yield powerful outcomes. We crave human connection. Throughout history, presenter-to-audience exchanges have rallied revolutions, spread innovation, and spawned movements. **Presentations create a catalyst for meaningful change by using human contact in a way that no other medium can.** Many times it isn't until you speak with people in person that you can establish a visceral connection that motivates them to adopt your idea. **That connection is why average ideas sometimes get traction and brilliant ideas die—it all comes down to how the ideas are presented.**

Presentations with a pulse have an ebb and flow to them. Those bursts of movement result from contrast—contrast in content, emotion, and delivery. In the same way that your toe taps to a good beat, your brain enjoys tapping into ideas when something new is continually developing and unwrapping. Interesting insights and contrasts keep the audience leaning forward, waiting to hear how each new development resolves.

It takes a lot of work to breathe life into an idea. Creating an interesting presentation requires a more thoughtful process than throwing together the blather that we've come to call a presentation today. Spending energy to understand the audience and carefully crafting a message that resonates with them means making a commitment of time and discipline to the process.

There is a simple way to determine whether it's worth putting this level of commitment into a presentation...

Just ask yourself: How badly do I want my idea to live?

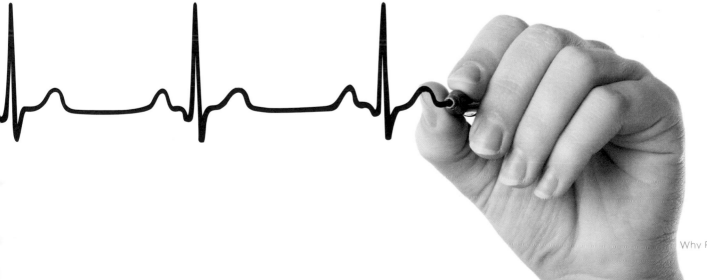

The Bland Leading the Bland

The presenter's job is to make the audience clearly "see" ideas. If your ideas stand out, they'll be noticed.

The enemy of persuasion is obscurity.

You can learn what attracts attention by examining the opposite: camouflage. The purpose of camouflage is to reduce the odds that someone will notice you—by blending into an environment. When is blending in appropriate for a communicator? Never. The more you want your idea adopted, the more it must stand out. If the idea blends with the environment, both its clarity and chances for adoption are diminished. An audience should never be asked to make decisions based on unclear options.

Don't blend in; instead, clash with your environment. Stand out. Be uniquely different. That's what will draw attention to your ideas. Nothing has intrinsic attention-grabbing power in itself. The power lies in how much something stands out from its context. If you go hunting with your college buddies and don't want to be confused with their prey, you'd be advised to wear safety orange. Since there's nothing in the woods that particular color, you'll stand out.

In communications, standing out from the "environment" means standing out among your competitors or even contrasting with your own organization. You must show how your idea contrasts with existing expectations, beliefs, feelings, or attitudes if you want to gain the audience's rapt attention. It certainly feels safer and easier to conform to the well-worn groove of sameness than to stand out and be vulnerable. But being buried in a sea of sameness does not yield greatness or solve big problems.

It can be scary running around your bland organization with a safety orange target on your back. It's risky, and it takes fortitude to be different among friends and foes. But it's important for your message to stand out, or it won't be remembered.

While you don't necessarily need to rebel against the current messages and content, you do need to lift them out of the drab, traditional way they are communicated. Identify opportunities for contrast and then create fascination and passion around these contrasts. Presentations today are boring because there is nothing interesting happening. They have no contrast, and hence interest is lost.

People Are Interesting

A great way to stand out is to be real. Presentations tend to be stripped of all humanness—despite the fact that humans make up the entire audience! Many corporations condition employees to put meaningless words together, project them on a slide, and talk about them like an automaton. The cultural norm is for presenters to hide behind slides as though that's a form of skilled communication. Look at the slides to the right. These are real statements taken from real presentations. They're meaningless. Yet these statements were written to attract and lure customers to products or services. It's the wrong bait.

Presenters think they can hide behind a wall of jargon, but what people are really looking for at a presentation is some kind of human connection.

By far the most human, transparent, and relational form of communication takes place when two people share common beliefs and create a connection based on beliefs. A presentation is an ideal opportunity for connecting because it's one of the few forms of interaction in which people are involved with one another *in person.*

Deep connections are what make a great presentation stand out. **Forming connections is an art, and when it's practiced well, the results can be astounding.**

Being human and taking risks are the foundation of creative results. Taking risks shows you're willing to tap into something your gut is telling you will work, without letting your head talk you out of it. That's creativity and humanness at its best. Unfortunately, many cultures stifle risk-taking, and many workplaces constrain human connectedness.

"Being true to yourself involves showing and sharing emotion. The spirit that motivates most great storytellers is 'I want you to feel what I feel,' and the effective narrative is designed to make this happen. That's how the information is bound to the experience and rendered unforgettable."

Peter Guber[1]

It's easier to rattle off jargon and keep communication emotionally neutral. But easiest doesn't always mean best.

These statements are from real presentations that have had all the humanness sucked out of them. It's easier to hide behind messages like these instead of tapping into what is human about us.

At XYZ Co. we create new, innovative businesses that would minimize the return-on-investment period for both strategic and financial investors, while experiencing significant revenue expansion.

XYZ Co. is an international company of more than twenty talented professionals dedicated to maximizing sales opportunities and revenues throughout Europe and North America for quality media owners with leading online and/or print brands.

XYZ Co. improves quality of life by improving capability maturity.

XYZ Co. creates the ultimate global alliance to monetize the Internet. We are the most reliable partner for global performance-based multichannel commerce, offering best-of-breed technology, services, and network to make more money with the Internet.

XYZ Co. is an online global resource center and membership community dedicated to helping small-business owners succeed and prosper.

XYZ Co. delivers to our clients their design team's intent and vision, at the lowest overall total delivered costs, with no sacrifice in quality, on time, and at, or more typically below budget.

XYZ Co. creates a center for rapid prototyping of innovations that encourage rapid failures to create innovations of all kinds that create both an inbound and outbound gradient.

XYZ Co. enriches lives with superior products at exceptional prices.

XYZ Co. provides every athlete — from professional to recreational runners to kids on the playground—with the opportunity, products, and inspiration to do great things. XYZ Co. helps consumers, athletes, artists, partners, and employees reach heights they may have thought unreachable.

Facts Alone Fall Short

You can have piles of facts and still fail to resonate. It's not the information itself that's important but the emotional impact of that information. This doesn't mean that you should abandon facts entirely. Use plenty of facts, but accompany them with emotional appeal.

There's a difference between being convinced with logic and believing with personal conviction. Your audience may agree with the thought process you present, but they still might not respond to the call. People rarely act by reason alone. You need to tap into other deeply seated desires and beliefs in order to be persuasive. You need a small thorn that is sharper than fact to prick their hearts. That thorn is emotion.

"The problem is this: No spreadsheet, no bibliography and no list of resources is sufficient proof to someone who chooses not to believe. The skeptic will always find a reason, even if it's one the rest of us don't think is a good one. Relying too much on proof distracts you from the real mission—which is emotional connection."

Seth Godin[2]

At some point in your life, you've had your emotions aroused. You've experienced a chill down your spine or a sick feeling in the pit of your stomach. When something resonates emotionally, you feel it physically.

Currently, emotion is a powerful driver of consumer behavior, but it didn't used to be. Before the 1900s, people rarely expressed emotion publicly; it was not socially acceptable to discuss feelings or desires. Products developed were solely marketed as items of necessity, not items of *desire*. As PR and advertising became prevalent, companies began to compete based on consumer desire and not necessarily consumer need. Suddenly, irrelevant objects became powerful symbols of status.

Today, appealing to emotion is commonplace. Ads can make us laugh or cry, feel sexy or feel guilty. A full range of emotions can be felt during one thirty-minute television show. Even restaurant menus tantalize us with food that will make us feel decadent, surprised, or enraptured. We can't escape it.

So today more than ever, communicating only the detailed specifications or functional overviews of a product isn't enough. **If two products have the same features, the one that appeals to an emotional need will be chosen.**

Aristotle said that the man who is in command of persuasion must be able "to understand the emotions—that is, to name them and describe them, to know their causes and the way in which they are excited," and that "persuasion may come through the hearers, when the speech stirs their emotions."[3]

Consumers are accustomed to emotional appeal, and they are most certainly ready to respond emotionally to a presentation. So why don't we present emotion? It's uncomfortable. It's an especially tough skill for analytical professionals to adopt. It's easy to think, "I don't get paid at work to *feel*, I get paid to *do*." And that's true. But if your team isn't motivated to move forward or your customers aren't motivated to buy, then you are in trouble.

Including emotion in a presentation doesn't mean it should be half fact and half emotion. It also doesn't mean there should be boxes of tissue under each seat. It simply means that you introduce humanness that appeals to the desires of the audience. It's not that difficult to evoke a visceral reaction in an audience if you use stories.

"The public is composed of numerous groups whose cry to us writers is: 'Comfort me.' 'Amuse me.' 'Touch my sympathies.' 'Make me sad.' 'Make me dream.' 'Make me laugh.' 'Make me shiver.' 'Make me weep.' 'Make me think.'"

Henri René Albert Guy do Maupassant[4]

Stories Convey Meaning

Ever since humans first sat around the campfire, stories have been told to create emotional connections. In many societies, they have been passed along nearly unchanged for generations. The greatest stories of all time were packaged and transferred so well that hundreds of illiterate generations could repeat them. Our early ancestors had stories to explain day-to-day occurrences in nature such as why the sun rises and falls, as well as more overarching metanarratives about the meaning of life. **Stories are the most powerful delivery tool for information, more powerful and enduring than any other art form.**

People love stories because life is full of adventure and we're hardwired to learn lessons from observing change in others. Life is messy, so we empathize with characters who have real-life challenges similar to the ones we face. When we listen to a story, the chemicals in our body change, and our mind becomes transfixed.[5] We are riveted when a character encounters a situation that involves risks and elated when he averts danger and is rewarded.

If you're like many professionals, using stories to create emotional appeal feels unnatural because it requires showing at least some degree of vulnerability to people you don't personally know all *that* well. Telling a personal story can be especially daunting because great personal stories have a conflict or complication that exposes your humanness or flaws. But these are also the stories that have the most inherent power to change others. People enjoy following a leader who has survived personal challenges and can share her narrative of struggle and victory (or defeat) comfortably.

"The best way to unite an idea with an emotion is by telling a compelling story. In a story, you not only weave a lot of information into the telling but you also arouse your listener's emotions and energy. Persuading with a story is hard. Any intelligent person can sit down and make lists. It takes rationality but little creativity to design an argument using conventional rhetoric. But it demands vivid insight and storytelling skill to present an idea that packs enough emotional power to be memorable. If you can harness imagination and the principles of a well-told story, then you get people rising to their feet amid thunderous applause instead of yawning and ignoring you."

Robert McKee[6]

Information is static; stories are dynamic—they help an audience visualize what you do or what you believe. Tell a story and people will be more engaged and receptive to the ideas you are communicating. **Stories link one person's heart to another. Values, beliefs, and norms become intertwined. When this happens, your idea can more readily manifest as reality in their minds.**

Campfires have been replaced with projector bulbs, and the power of story has eluded presenters in the workplace.

You Are Not the Hero

When trying to connect with others during a presentation, you have to remember that it's not *all* about you. Audiences detest arrogance and self-centeredness. They evoke the same feeling you get when you arrive at a party only to be cornered by a dreadful, self-centered know-it-all. He'll talk about his own interests, how cool he is, and how great he is while you're left thinking, "What an ass," and looking for any opportunity to get away. Why is that? It's because the conversation doesn't include you, your ideas, or your perspective. **Self-centered people don't connect. No one wants to date, work with, or sit through a presentation given by someone like that.** So why are presentations rife with self-centered content?

It's all about me

I'm best of breed

My partners are cool

I have synergy

I'm great!

Customers & analysts LOVE me

My product is the best

I'm available 24/7

Let's talk more about me

My market cap is HUGE

I have lots of employees in many locations

You need my help

I'm flexible & scalable

I'm in a win-win situation

Most presentations start with "me-ness." Somewhere in the front of the slide deck is the dreaded "it's all about me" slide that typically looks like one of the slides to the right.

It is important that the audience know something about you and your company. There are other ways to communicate this information (like a handout) so you can focus on the people in the audience right at the onset and focus your presentation so it resonates at their frequency instead of yours.

As a presenter, it's easy to feel like your product or cause should be the most important thing on the minds of the audience. You may even think, "I'm their hero, here to save them from their helplessness and ignorance. If they only knew what I know, the world would be a better place." If you show up and chatter about yourself, your products, and your synergies, you will become the self-centered know-it-all at the party, and the audience will want to flee.

Instead, embrace a stance of humility and deference to your audience's needs. Begin the presentation from a shared place of understanding.

Make it about the audience.

SELFISH APPROACH

- About us
  - Company history
  - Market cap
  - # employees and # locations
- About our product and service
  - What it is
  - How it works
  - Why it's better than the alternative
- Call to action (ideally)

SAMPLES FROM BAD PRESENTATIONS

XYZ Co. Equity Partners, LLC

- Founded in 1988 in Anchorage, Alaska
- Invest in companies who:
  - Provide professional IT services
  - Offer exceptional technical and project management expertise
  - Deliver complex data and information management solutions as systems and/or applications integrators
- Average annual revenue: $51.5M

XYZ Co. Software

- Established in 1984
- Headquarters: San Francisco, CA
- Integrated P&C Insurance software and services
- Focused on Alternative Risk & Self-Insured markets
- Recognized leader in risk management solutions
- Over 100 customers in U.S. and Canada

The Audience Is the Hero

You need to defer to your audience because if they don't engage and believe in your message, you are the one who loses. Without their help, your idea will fail.

You are not the hero who will save the audience; the audience is your hero.

Screenwriter Chad Hodge points out in *Harvard Business Review* that we should "[help] people to see themselves as the hero of the story, whether the plot involves beating the bad guys or achieving some great business objective. Everyone wants to be a star, or at least to feel that the story is talking to or about him personally."[7] Business leaders need to take this to heart, place the people in the audience at the center of the action, and make them feel that the presentation is addressing them personally.

When you're presenting, instead of showing up with an arrogant attitude that "it's all about me," your stance should be a humble "it's all about them." Remember, the success of you and your firm is dependent on them, not the other way around. You need them.

So what's your role then? You are the mentor. You're Yoda, not Luke Skywalker. The audience is the one who'll do all the heavy lifting to help you reach your objectives. You're simply one voice helping them get unstuck in their journey.

The mentor is often personified as a wise person such as The Oracle in *The Matrix* or even Mr. Miyagi in *The Karate Kid*. As mentor, your role is to give the hero guidance, confidence, insight, advice, training, or magical gifts so he can overcome his initial fears and enter into the new journey with you.

Changing your stance from thinking you're the hero to acknowledging your role as mentor will alter your viewpoint. You'll come from a place of humility, the aide-de-camp to your audience. A mentor has a selfless nature and is willing to make personal sacrifices so that the hero can reach the reward.

Most mentors were heroes themselves. They have become experienced enough to teach others about the special tools or powers they picked up on the journey of their own lives. Mentors have been down the road of the hero one or more times and have acquired skills that can be passed on to the hero.

When you step up to give your presentation, you might be the most knowledgeable person in the room, but will you wield that knowledge with wisdom and humility? Presentations are not to be viewed as an opportunity to prove how brilliant you are. Instead, the audience should leave saying, "Wow, it was a real gift to spend time in that presentation with (insert your name here). I'm armed with insights and tools to help me succeed that I didn't have before."

Changing your stance from hero to mentor will clothe you in humility and help you see things from a new perspective. **Audience insights and resonance can only occur when a presenter takes a stance of humility.**

The audience is the hero.

That's you!

Luke Skywalker and Yoda
Star Wars: Episode V—The Empire Strikes Back

Presentations have the power to change the world. The nexus of almost every movement and high-stakes decision relies on the spoken word to get traction, and presentations are a powerful platform to persuade.

But presentations are broken; they are considered a necessary evil instead of a tool of great power. That power springs from the presenter's ability to make a deep human connection with others. Instead of connecting with others, presentations tend to be self-centered, which alienates audiences. The opportunity to transform is diminished when audiences don't feel a connection.

Changing your stance from that of the hero to one of wise storyteller will connect the audience to your idea, and an audience connected to your idea will change.

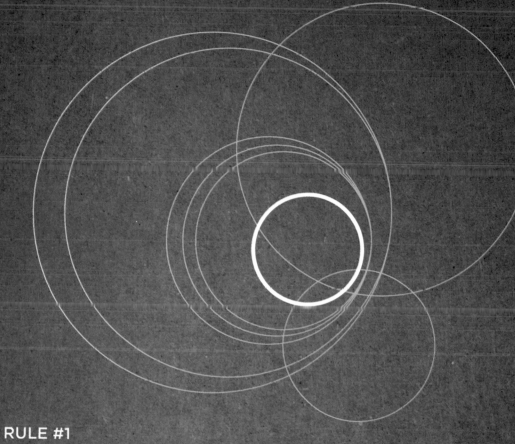

Resonance causes change.

CHAPTER 2

Lessons from Myths and Movies

Incorporate Story

All types of writing, including presentations, fall somewhere in between two extreme poles: reports and stories. Reports inform, while stories entertain. The structural difference between a report and a story is that a report organizes facts by topic, while a story organizes scenes dramatically.[1] Presentations fall in the middle and contain both information and story, so they are called explanations.

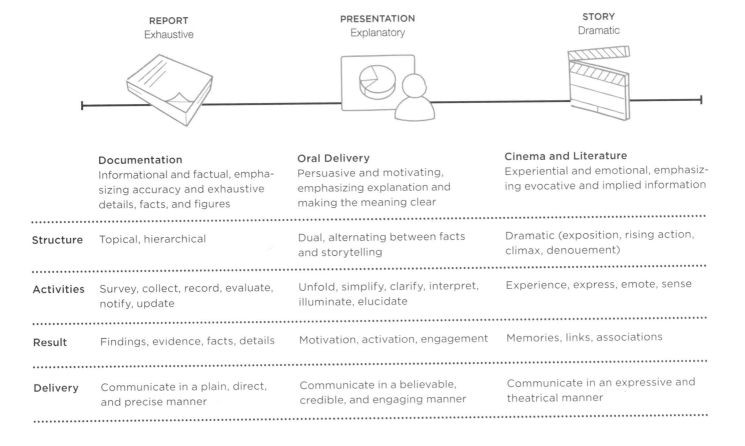

	REPORT Exhaustive	**PRESENTATION** Explanatory	**STORY** Dramatic
	Documentation Informational and factual, emphasizing accuracy and exhaustive details, facts, and figures	**Oral Delivery** Persuasive and motivating, emphasizing explanation and making the meaning clear	**Cinema and Literature** Experiential and emotional, emphasizing evocative and implied information
Structure	Topical, hierarchical	Dual, alternating between facts and storytelling	Dramatic (exposition, rising action, climax, denouement)
Activities	Survey, collect, record, evaluate, notify, update	Unfold, simplify, clarify, interpret, illuminate, elucidate	Experience, express, emote, sense
Result	Findings, evidence, facts, details	Motivation, activation, engagement	Memories, links, associations
Delivery	Communicate in a plain, direct, and precise manner	Communicate in a believable, credible, and engaging manner	Communicate in an expressive and theatrical manner

It's become the cultural norm to write presentations as reports instead of stories. But presentations are not reports. Many people who create presentations are stuck in the mindset that if they use a presentation application, like PowerPoint, to create a report, the report is a presentation. It is not! Reports should be distributed; presentations should be presented. Documents masquerade as presentations, and these "slideuments"[2] have become the *lingua franca* of many organizations. While documents and reports are very valuable, they do not need to be projected for the purpose of hosting a "read-along."

So if a report primarily conveys *information,* then stories produce an *experience*. Blending the two creates a perfect world for your presentation where facts and stories can be layered like a cake. Navigating between fact, then story, then fact, then story creates interest and a pulse. Mixing report material with story material makes information more digestible. It's the sugar that helps the medicine go down.

It's more comfortable and less time consuming to present flat, data-driven static reports, but that approach doesn't connect people to ideas. The moment you know you need to create a presentation and not a report, shift your mindset from solely transferring information to creating an experience. This is the first step in moving along the spectrum away from a pure report toward a story.

There are plenty of opportunities to use dramatic story structure in presentations. But how do you create a dramatic experience? **Creating desire in the audience and then showing how your ideas fill that desire moves people to adopt your perspective. This is the heart of a story.**

This chapter will draw insights from the best story methods available today: mythology, literature, and cinema. Once you understand their power, you'll see why great presentations move away from reports and closer to stories.

Drama Is Everything

Presentations have the potential to hold an audience's interest just like a good movie. You might be thinking that it takes years to write a successful screenplay, and you have a real job to do. But isn't part of your "real job" to communicate ideas well, help people understand objectives, and persuade them to change? Building your presentations with some of the attributes from myths and movies will help your ideas resonate with others.

Great stories introduce you to a hero to whom you can relate. The hero is usually a likeable sort who has an acute desire or goal that is threatened in some way. As the story unfolds and trials are met with triumph, you cheer for the hero until the story is resolved and the hero is transformed. As author Robert McKee explains, "Something must be at stake that convinces the audience that a great deal will be lost if the hero doesn't obtain his goal."[3] If nothing is at risk, then it's not interesting.

Your communications follow a similar pattern. You have a goal that needs to be reached, but there will be trials and resistance. However, when your desire is realized, the outcome will yield remarkable results.

One of the reasons presentations are dull is because there are no identifiable story patterns. In the next few pages, you'll review story models actively used in Hollywood that are fundamental to a good screenplay. These forms work! They are not formulas or rigid sets of rules—they address structure and character transformation, yet also leave room for flexibility and creativity. After you review the Hollywood story forms, you'll be introduced to the presentation form. It's a similar form, but one that's tailored to presentations. Applying these methods will help craft your message and unlock the story potential in your presentations.

Story Pattern

The most simplistic way to describe the structure of a story is situation, complication, and resolution. From mythic adventures to recollections shared around the dinner table, all stories follow this pattern.

RELATABLE AND LIKABLE HERO	ENCOUNTERS ROADBLOCKS	EMERGES TRANSFORMED
Snow White **Situation:** Snow White takes refuge in the forest with seven dwarfs to hide from her stepmother, the wicked queen.	**Complication:** Snow White is more beautiful than her stepmother so, disguised as a peddler, she poisons Snow White with an apple.	**Resolution:** The prince, who has fallen in love with Snow White, awakens her from the spell with "love's first kiss."
E.T. **Situation:** A group of alien botanists visit earth. After a hasty takeoff, one of them is left behind. And he wants to get back home.	**Complication:** Ten-year-old Elliott forms an emotional bond with E.T., a task force tries to hunt down E.T., and he and Elliott get very sick.	**Resolution:** E.T. and Elliott build a communication device and escape on a bicycle. E.T. is rescued and tells Elliott he'll be in his heart.
Avatar **Situation:** Jake Sully is a paralyzed ex-Marine who is selected for the Avatar program, which will enable him to walk through a proxy Na'vi body in the land of Pandora.	**Complication:** Jake falls in love with a Na'vi woman, Neytiri, in Pandora. As the humans encroach on the forest seeking valuable minerals, Jake is forced to choose sides in an epic battle.	**Resolution:** Under Jake's leadership, the Na'vi defeat the humans. Jake is permanently transformed into a Na'vi and gets to live on Pandora with Neytiri.

Story Templates Create Structure

Screenwriters use tools to create strong story stuctures. Syd Field is considered the father of Hollywood's story template. In his book, *Screenplay,* Field uses concepts from the three-act structure first proposed by Aristotle to create the Syd Field Paradigm, shown on the right. Field noticed that in successful movies, the second act was often twice the length of the first and third acts:

- **Act 1** sets up the story by introducing characters, creating relationships, and establishing the hero's unfulfilled desire, which holds the plot in place.

- **Act 2** presents dramatic action held together by confrontation. The main character encounters obstacles that keep him or her from achieving his or her desire (dramatic need).

- **Act 3** resolves the story. Resolution doesn't mean ending but rather *solution.* Did the main character succeed or fail?[4]

All stories have a beginning, middle, and an end. There's a defining point in which the beginning turns into the middle and the middle into the end. Field, a leading screenwriting teacher, calls these *plot points.* A plot point is defined as any incident, episode, or event that spins the story around in another direction. Each plot point sets up the story for a change.

A great presentation is similar to a screenplay in several ways:

- It has a clear beginning, middle, and end.

- It has an identifiable, inherent structure.

- The first plot point is an incident that captures the audience's intrigue and interest. In presentations, we'll call this a *turning point.*

- The beginning and end are much shorter than the middle.

This is a form, not a formula. It's what a screenplay would look like if you could X-ray it and examine its structure. The movie *Shawshank Redemption** is shown to the right with the acts and plot points annotated.

Field's model makes sense as a template for scripting movies; however, it is only partially applicable to presentations. Next, we'll examine an additional story form that will supply some of the missing pieces.

Syd Field's Paradigm[5]

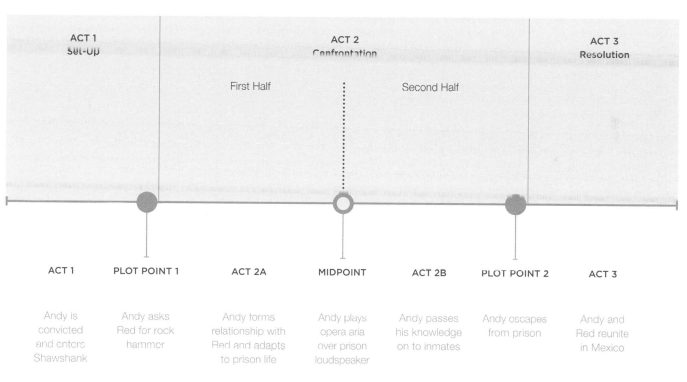

| ACT 1 | | ACT 2 | | | | ACT 3 |
| Set-Up | | Confrontation | | | | Resolution |

First Half · Second Half

ACT 1	PLOT POINT 1	ACT 2A	MIDPOINT	ACT 2B	PLOT POINT 2	ACT 3
Andy is convicted and enters Shawshank	Andy asks Red for rock hammer	Andy forms relationship with Red and adapts to prison life	Andy plays opera aria over prison loudspeaker	Andy passes his knowledge on to inmates	Andy escapes from prison	Andy and Red reunite in Mexico

*SHAWSHANK REDEMPTION STORY

Andy, a young banker convicted of murdering his wife and her lover, is sentenced to Shawshank Penitentiary. In prison, Andy meets and forms a relationship with Red, another convicted killer, and then becomes an ally and trusted friend of the warden. When his attempts for a retrial fail, he escapes from Shawshank. At the end, Andy makes his way to Mexico, where he and Red are reunited.

The Hero's Journey Structure

Another story model to consider is *The Hero's Journey,* drawn from the psychology of Carl Jung and mythological studies of Joseph Campbell.

The wheel to the right is an overview of The Hero's Journey that has been slightly simplified by Christopher Vogler, author of *The Writer's Journey.* Vogler spent years as a story analyst for screenplays in Hollywood and uses this as a form for his analyses. Starting at the top of the wheel, move clockwise through the steps. The gray text of the innermost circle walks you through the stages of The Hero's Journey: (1) Heroes are introduced in the Ordinary World, where (2) they receive the Call to Adventure. (3) They are initially reluctant and might even Refuse the Call but (4) are encouraged by a Mentor to (5) Cross the First Threshold and enter the Special World, where (6) they encounter Tests, Allies, and Enemies. (7) They Approach the Inmost Cave, where (8) they endure the Ordeal. (9) They take possession of their Reward and (10) are pursued on the Road Back to the Ordinary World. (11) They experience a Resurrection and are transformed by the experience. (12) They Return with the Elixir—a boon or treasure to benefit the Ordinary World.[6]

Heroes endure physical activities (outer journey) but also experience internal transformations to their hearts and minds at each stage. This inner journey is represented by green text in the second ring. Then, the outermost ring uses *Star Wars: Episode IV* as an example, showing the outer journey in gray text and the inner journey in green.

An important insight emerges when The Hero's Journey is represented in a circle: It creates a clear division between the *ordinary world* and the *special world* (signified by the gray dotted line). **There is a moment in every story where the character overcomes reluctance to change, leaves the ordinary world, and crosses the threshold into an adventure in a special world.** In the special world, the hero gains skills and insights—and then brings them back to the ordinary world as the story resolves.

A good presentation is a satisfying, complete experience. You might cry, laugh, or do both, but you'll also feel you've learned something about yourself.

Presentations use insights from myths and movies in several ways:

- There's a likable yet flawed hero attending your presentation.

- A presentation should take the audience on a journey from their ordinary world into your special world, gaining new insights and skills from your special world.

- The audience makes a conscious decision to cross the threshold into your world; they are not forced.

- The audience will resist adopting your point of view and will point out obstacles and roadblocks.

- The audience needs to change on the inside before they'll change on the outside. In other words, they need to alter their perception internally before they change the way they act.

Crossing the threshold is an important moment because it signals that the hero is making a commitment. Let's look more closely at that turning point.

The Hero's Journey

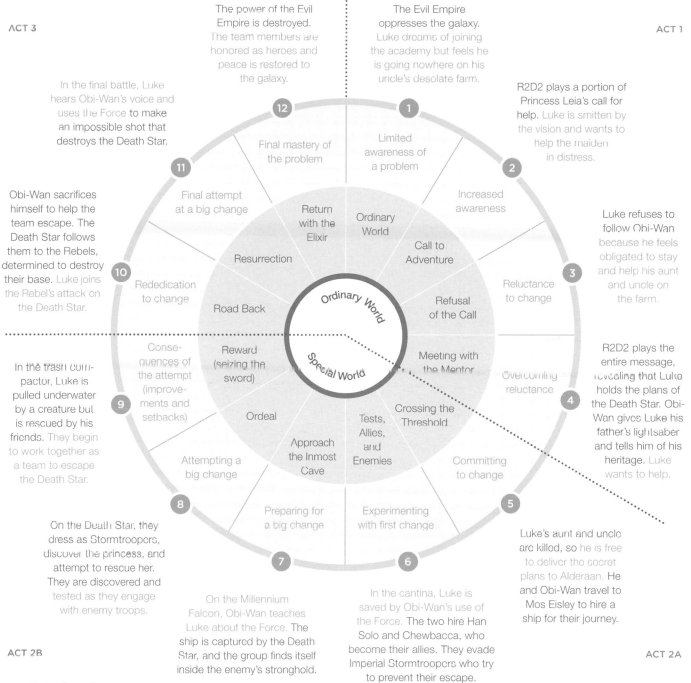

ACT 3

The power of the Evil Empire is destroyed. The team members are honored as heroes and peace is restored to the galaxy.

In the final battle, Luke hears Obi-Wan's voice and uses the Force to make an impossible shot that destroys the Death Star.

Obi-Wan sacrifices himself to help the team escape. The Death Star follows them to the Rebels, determined to destroy their base. Luke joins the Rebel's attack on the Death Star.

ACT 2B

In the trash compactor, Luke is pulled underwater by a creature but is rescued by his friends. They begin to work together as a team to escape the Death Star.

On the Death Star, they dress as Stormtroopers, discover the princess, and attempt to rescue her. They are discovered and tested as they engage with enemy troops.

On the Millennium Falcon, Obi-Wan teaches Luke about the Force. The ship is captured by the Death Star, and the group finds itself inside the enemy's stronghold.

ACT 1

The Evil Empire oppresses the galaxy. Luke dreams of joining the academy but feels he is going nowhere on his uncle's desolate farm.

R2D2 plays a portion of Princess Leia's call for help. Luke is smitten by the vision and wants to help the maiden in distress.

Luke refuses to follow Obi-Wan because he feels obligated to stay and help his aunt and uncle on the farm.

R2D2 plays the entire message, revealing that Luke holds the plans of the Death Star. Obi-Wan gives Luke his father's lightsaber and tells him of his heritage. Luke wants to help.

Luke's aunt and uncle are killed, so he is free to deliver the secret plans to Alderaan. He and Obi-Wan travel to Mos Eisley to hire a ship for their journey.

ACT 2A

In the cantina, Luke is saved by Obi-Wan's use of the Force. The two hire Han Solo and Chewbacca, who become their allies. They evade Imperial Stormtroopers who try to prevent their escape.

Outer ring (numbered stages)

1. Limited awareness of a problem
2. Increased awareness
3. Reluctance to change
4. Overcoming reluctance
5. Committing to change
6. Experimenting with first change
7. Preparing for a big change
8. Attempting a big change
9. Consequences of the attempt (improvements and setbacks)
10. Rededication to change
11. Final attempt at a big change
12. Final mastery of the problem

Inner ring

- Ordinary World
- Call to Adventure
- Refusal of the Call
- Meeting with the Mentor
- Crossing the Threshold
- Tests, Allies, and Enemies
- Approach the Inmost Cave
- Ordeal
- Reward (seizing the sword)
- Road Back
- Resurrection
- Return with the Elixir

Center

Ordinary World
Special World

gray text = inner journey

green text = outer journey (character transformation)

Factoid: When George Lucas came across Joseph Campbell's work, he modified *Star Wars, Episode IV* to map more closely to this model.

Crossing the Threshold

If the audience is the hero in your story, then the objective during your presentation is to get them past the fourth step in the wheel. Your presentation takes them to the threshold, but it's their choice whether to cross it or not.

Your presentation proposes an idea, and you're asking the audience to adopt and shepherd that idea to positive outcomes. Your idea might be to reshape an organization for the future or to show customers how your product will fill a need they have. It might even be to have students test well and internalize the subject matter. Whatever it is, the decisions the audience might make require them to consciously step into something new.

The change you're requesting will not come without a struggle for your heroes—and you need to acknowledge that. Change is hard. Getting people to commit to change is probably an organization's greatest challenge. Notice how the hero meets the mentor *just* when he or she needs to decide whether to cross the threshold—and enter the special world. It's a lovely parallel to presenting. As their mentor, your insights will help the audience make a decision to change. But you can't force them. If you present well, they'll cross the threshold voluntarily and jump in.

If the audience has decided to cross the threshold and adopt your perspective, they begin the rest of The Hero's Journey (stages five through twelve) when they leave your presentation. As their mentor, your presentation should prepare them as much as possible for what they can expect on the rest of the journey and set them up to be successful along the way. Usually, the stages of The Hero's Journey in movies take place in sequential, chronological order. But when developing a presentation, you aren't bound to keep to the constraints of a place and time. The presentation medium allows you to bounce around out of sequence as you address insights into how steps five to twelve will be accomplished.

Let's remember that there is one indisputable attribute of a good story: **there must be some kind of conflict or imbalance perceived by the audience that your presentation resolves.** This sense of discord is what persuades them to care enough to jump in. In a presentation, you create imbalance by consciously juxtaposing *what is* with *what could be.*

Clearly contrast who the audience is when they walk into the room (in their ordinary world) with whom they could be when they leave the room (crossing the threshold into a special world). *What is* versus *what could be.* Drawing attention to that gap forces the audience to contend with the imbalance until a new balance is achieved.

The Audience's Journey

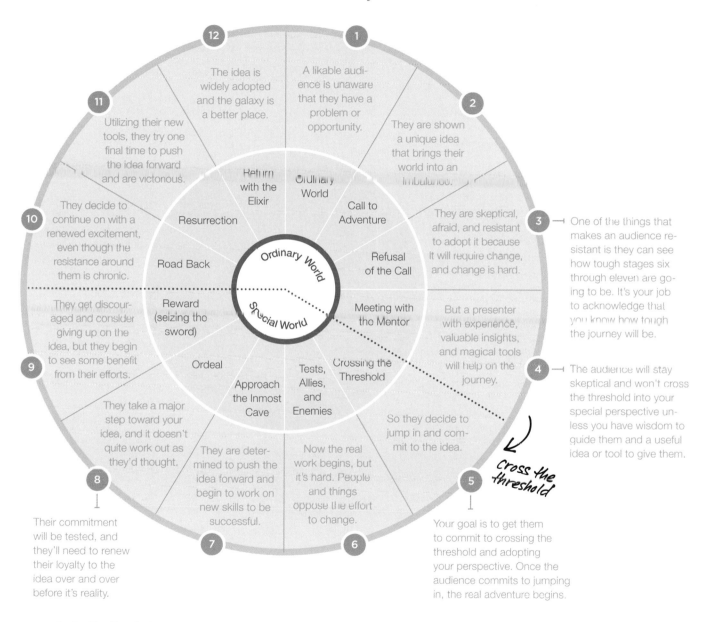

A likable audience is unaware that they have a problem or opportunity.

They are shown a unique idea that brings their world into an imbalance.

They are skeptical, afraid, and resistant to adopt it because it will require change, and change is hard.

One of the things that makes an audience resistant is they can see how tough stages six through eleven are going to be. It's your job to acknowledge that you know how tough the journey will be.

But a presenter with experience, valuable insights, and magical tools will help on the journey.

The audience will stay skeptical and won't cross the threshold into your special perspective unless you have wisdom to guide them and a useful idea or tool to give them.

So they decide to jump in and commit to the idea.

Cross the threshold

Your goal is to get them to commit to crossing the threshold and adopting your perspective. Once the audience commits to jumping in, the real adventure begins.

Now the real work begins, but it's hard. People and things oppose the effort to change.

They are determined to push the idea forward and begin to work on new skills to be successful.

Their commitment will be tested, and they'll need to renew their loyalty to the idea over and over before it's reality.

They take a major step toward your idea, and it doesn't quite work out as they'd thought.

They get discouraged and consider giving up on the idea, but they begin to see some benefit from their efforts.

They decide to continue on with a renewed excitement, even though the resistance around them is chronic.

Utilizing their new tools, they try one final time to push the idea forward and are victorious.

The idea is widely adopted and the galaxy is a better place.

Inner ring (gray text — The Hero's Journey): Ordinary World, Call to Adventure, Refusal of the Call, Meeting with the Mentor, Crossing the Threshold, Tests, Allies, and Enemies, Approach the Inmost Cave, Ordeal, Reward (seizing the sword), Road Back, Resurrection, Return with the Elixir

Center: Ordinary World / Special World

gray text = The Hero's Journey
blue text = the audience's journey

The Contour of Communication
The Presentation Form

Drawing insights from mythological, literary, and cinematic structures, a *presentation form* emerged. Most great presentations unknowingly follow this form.

Presentations should have a clear beginning, middle, and end. Two clear turning points in a presentation's structure guide the audience through the content and distinctively separate the beginning from the middle and the middle from the end. The first is the *call to adventure*—this should show the audience a gap between *what is* and *what could be*—jolting the audience from complacency. When effectively constructed—an imbalance is created—the audience will want your presentation to resolve this imbalance. The second turning point is the *call to action,* which identifies what the audience needs to do or how they need to change. This second turning point signifies that you're coming to the presentation's conclusion.

Notice how the middle moves up and down as if something new is happening continually. This back and forth structural motion pushes and pulls the audience to feel as if events are constantly unfolding. An audience will stay engaged as you unwrap ideas and perspectives frequently.

Each presentation concludes with a vivid description of the *new bliss* that's created when your audience adopts your proposed idea. But notice that the presentation form doesn't stop at the end of the presentation. Presentations are meant to persuade, so there is also a subsequent action (or crossing the threshold) the audience is to do once they leave the presentation.

Let's look at the form in more detail on the following pages.

BEGINNING

Paint a picture of the realities of the audience's current world.

What could be

The gap

What is

What is

Turning Point 1

CALL TO ADVENTURE

Create an imbalance by stating *what could be* juxtaposed to *what is.*

MIDDLE

Present contrasting content, alternating
between *what is* and *what could be*.

END

End the presentation
on a higher plane than
it began, with every-
one understanding the
reward in the future.

CROSS THE THRESHOLD

The audience leaves the
presentation committed to taking
action, knowing it won't be easy
but will be worth the reward.

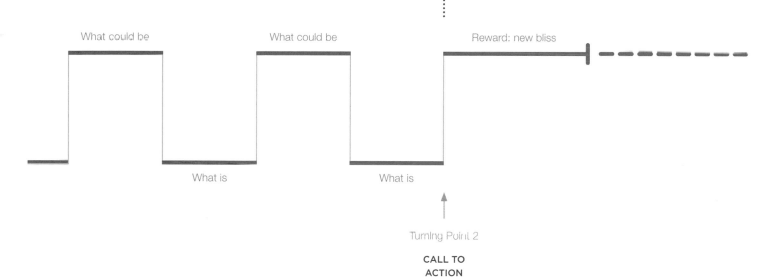

What could be

What could be

Reward: new bliss

What is

What is

Turning Point 2

**CALL TO
ACTION**

Articulate the finish line
the audience is to cross.

The Beginning and Call to Adventure

The Hero's Journey begins when "a hero ventures forth from the world of common day into a region of supernatural wonder."[7] Your presentation may not offer "supernatural wonder," but you are asking the audience to leave their comfort zone and venture to a new place that is closer to where you think they should be.

The beginning of the presentation form is everything that comes before the first turning point, the *call to adventure*. The first flat line of the form represents the beginning of your presentation. This is where you describe the audience's ordinary world and set the baseline of *what is*. You can use historical information about what has been or the current state of *what is,* which often includes the problem you're currently facing.

You should deliver a concise formulation of what everyone agrees is true. Accurately capturing the current reality and sentiments of the audience's world demonstrates that you have experience and insights on their situation and that you understand their perspective, context, and values.

Done effectively, this description of where your audience currently *is* will create a common bond between you and them and will open them up to hear your unique perspective more readily. Audiences are grateful when their contribution, intelligence, and experience are acknowledged.

Additionally, describing their existing world gives you the opportunity to create a dramatic dichotomy between *what is* and *what could be*. Proposing *what could be* should throw the audience's current reality out of balance. Without first setting up *what is,* the dramatic effect of your new idea will be lost.

The beginning doesn't have to be long. It might be as simple as a short statement or phrase that sets the baseline of *what is*. While it can be longer, it should not take up more than 10 percent of your total time. The audience will be anxious to know why they came and what you are proposing. So, although the beginning is important, it shouldn't be long-winded.

The first turning point to occur in a presentation is the call to adventure, which triggers a significant shift in the content. The call to adventure asks the audience to jump into a situation that, unbeknownst to them, requires their attention and action. This moment sets the presentation in motion.

"A bad beginning makes a bad ending."

Euripides[8]

To create the call to adventure, put forth a memorable big idea that conveys *what could be*. This is the moment when the audience will see the stark contrast between *what is* and *what could be* for the first time—and it's crucial that the gap is clear.

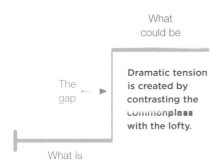

What could be

Dramatic tension is created by contrasting the commonplace with the lofty.

The gap ▶

What is

The call to adventure in a presentation plays a role similar to the *inciting incident* in a movie. *Story* author Robert McKee says, "The inciting incident first throws the protagonist's life out of balance, then arouses in him the desire to restore that balance."[9] That imbalance is what elicits the audience's desire for a reality different from the current one. Pose an intriguing insight that your audience will want the presentation to address. It should stir them up enough (positively or negatively) so that they want to listen intently as you explain what is at stake and what it takes to resolve the gap.

This turning point should be explicit, not muddled or vague. The remainder of the presentation should be about filling that gap and drawing the audience toward your unique perspective of *what could be*.

"Man is the only animal that laughs and weeps; for he is the only animal that is struck with the difference between what things are and what they ought to be."

William Hazlitt[10]

BELOW IS AN EXAMPLE OF A CALL TO ADVENTURE FOR A PRODUCT LAUNCH

What is: Analysts have been placing our products in the top spot in three out of five categories. Our competitor just shook up the industry with the launch of their T3xR. It has been heralded as the most innovative product in our space for the last four years. The predictions are that firms like ours will have no future unless we license the T3xR from our competitor.

What could be: But we will not concede! In fact, today we will retain our lead! I'm pleased to tell you that five years ago we had the same product idea as the T3xR. But after rapid prototyping we discovered a way to leapfrog that generation of technology. So today, we're launching a product so revolutionary that we'll gain a ten-year lead over our competitors. Ladies and gentlemen, introducing the e-Widget. Isn't it beautiful?

The Middle: Contrast

The middle of a presentation is made up of various types of contrast. People are naturally drawn to contrast because life is surrounded by it. Day and night. Male and female. Up and down. Good and evil. Love and hate.

Your job as a communicator is to create and resolve tension through contrast.

Building highly contrasting elements into a presentation holds the audience's attention. Audiences enjoy experiencing a dilemma and its resolution—even if that dilemma is caused by a viewpoint that's opposed to their own. It keeps them interested.

The audience wants to know if your views are similar to or different from their views. While listening to a presenter, audience members catalog and classify what they hear. Having come into the room with their own knowledge, and biases, they are constantly evaluating whether what you say fits within their life experiences or falls outside of what they know.

It's important to know your audience so that you can understand how your views are both similar to and different from theirs. There will usually be some disparities. A rather obvious business example would be that you want them to buy your product, and they don't want to spend the money.

But differences aren't a *problem.* The polarity between similar and dissimilar concepts creates a force that can be put to good use. In fact, both extremes are necessary

in a presentation. They allow you to create observable distinctions between your perspectives and your audience's perspectives—this helps keep their attention. Though people are generally more comfortable with what's familiar to them, conveying the opposite creates internal tension. **Oppositional content is stimulating; familiar content is comforting. Together, these two types of content produce forward movement.**

There are three distinct types of contrast you can build into a presentation:

- **Content:** Content contrast moves back and forth to compare *what is* to *what could be*—and your views versus the audience's (pages 104 to 105).

- **Emotion:** Emotional contrast moves back and forth between analytical and emotional content (pages 136 to 137).

- **Delivery:** Delivery contrast moves back and forth between traditional and nontraditional delivery methods (pages 138 to 139).

Contrast is a motif woven throughout this entire book and is at the heart of communication, because people are attracted to things that stand out.

"As the polarized nature of magnetic fields can be used to generate electrical energy, polarity in a story seems to be an engine that generates tension and movement in the characters and a stirring of emotions in the audience."

Chris Vogler[11]

Call to Action

The second turning point, the *call to action,* clearly defines what you're asking the audience to do. Successful persuasion leads to action, and it is important to clearly state exactly how you want the audience to take action. This step in the presentation gives the audience discrete tasks that will help bring the ideas you convey in your presentation to fruition. Once this line is crossed, the audience needs to decide if they are with you or not—so make it clear what needs to be accomplished.

Whether a presentation is political, corporate, or academic, the audience consists of four distinct types of people capable of taking action: doers, suppliers, influencers, and innovators.

Because of differences in temperaments, every audience member will have a natural preference for one type over another. Providing each type with at least one action that's suited to their temperament allows them to choose the action they're most comfortable performing. When audience members see how they can help, it leads to momentum and quicker results. Most people are equipped with the ability to carry out at least one of the four types of actions effectively. A truly passionate revolutionary for your ideas could embody all four of the action types.

Sample calls to action that can be requested of an audience:

- The doer can be asked to assemble, decide, gather, respond, or try.
- The supplier can be asked to acquire, fund, provide resources, or provide support.
- The influencer can be asked to activate, adopt, empower, or promote.
- The innovator can be asked to create, discover, invent, or pioneer.

Be sure to identify actions that are simple, straightforward, and easily executed. The audience should be able to mentally connect their actions with a positive outcome for themselves, or for the greater good. Present all the necessary actions and make sure the most critical tasks for success are emphasized.

Many presentations end with the call to action; however, ending a presentation with a to-do list for the audience is not inspirational. So it's important to follow up the call to action with a vivid picture of the potential reward.

WHO THEY ARE	**DOERS**	**SUPPLIERS**	**INFLUENCERS**	**INNOVATORS**
WHAT THEY DO FOR YOU	Instigate Activities	Get Resources	Change Perceptions	Generate Ideas
HOW THEY DO IT	These audience members are your worker bees. Once they know what has to be done, they'll do the physical tasks. They recruit and motivate other doers to complete important activities.	These audience members are the ones with the resources—financial, human, or material. They have the means to get you what you need to move forward.	These audience members can sway individuals and groups, large and small, mobilizing them to adopt and evangelize your idea.	These audience members think outside the box for new ways to modify and spread your idea. They create strategies, perspectives, and products. They bring their brains to the table.

The End

Notice that the end of the presentation is on a higher plane in the presentation form than the beginning. The ending should leave the audience with a heightened sense of *what could be* and a willingness to be transformed—to be able to either understand something new or do something differently. Audience transformation is the goal of persuasion. Skillfully defining the future reward compels the audience to get on board with your idea.

The ending should repeat the most important points and deliver inspirational remarks encompassing what the world will look like when your idea is adopted.

The principle of recency states that audiences remember the last content they heard in a presentation more vividly than the points made in the beginning or middle. So you should create an ending that describes an inspirational, blissful world—a world that has adopted your idea. What will the audience members' lives look like? What will humanity look like? What will the planet look like?

In order to get the most out of the audience, describe the possible future outcomes with wonder and awe. Show the audience that the reward will be worth their efforts. The presentation should conclude with the assertion that your idea is not only possible but that it is the right—and better—choice to make.

"Getting the audience to cheer, rise, and vocalize in response to a dramatic, rousing conclusion creates positive emotional contagion, produces a strong emotional takeaway, and fuels the call to action by the business leader. The ending of a great narrative is the first thing the audience remembers."

Peter Guber [12]

Let's say you pulled off an incredible presentation. You used the principles in the presentation form with grace and ease to convey your ideas, and the audience made a commitment to transform. Sounds like a huge victory—but it's not over yet. **The end of your presentation marks the next phase of the adventure for the audience.**

The human ability to accept new insights creates room for people to *become* something different. As indicated by the final dashed line at the end of the presentation form, the audience starts becoming something different from what they were at the beginning of the presentation.

But when you are done delivering your presentation, the adoption of your idea is still inconclusive. The audience will determine the outcome. Great presentations end with the audience leaving full of support; bad ones don't. The outcome could end as a comedy or as a tragedy. If they don't adopt your idea, it could end as a *tragedy* in which your once admirable hero makes a personal error by not moving forward with your call to action. Or if they do your call to action, it resolves as a *comedy,* which doesn't necessarily mean "funny"; it means there was a rise in the fortune of a hero who deserved to succeed.

"What we call the beginning is often the end. And to make an end is to make a beginning. The end is where we start from."

T. S. Eliot[13]

What Is a Sparkline?

Throughout this book, the presentation form will be used to analyze presentations graphically as a sparkline. This will help you see the contrast in a presentation by visualizing its contour. The line moves up and down between *what is* and *what could be,* but it also changes colors to signify contrasts in emotion and delivery. Each presentation has its own unique pattern. No two sparklines are alike, because no two presentations are alike.

Using a tool like the presentation form to achieve great results isn't new. Movies and myths all have a form, and they yield beautiful and unique results. Similarly,

presentations that follow the presentation form will all be unique. The presentation form isn't a formula, because it has enormous flexibility; rigid adherence to it could make your presentations too predictable. So it's equally important to embrace its versatility.

Below is an annotation of how to read the sparklines in the book. The case study on the following pages will show the first use of the presentation form applied as a sparkline. Videos of all the presentations analyzed are available online along with additional annotations to the transcripts. www

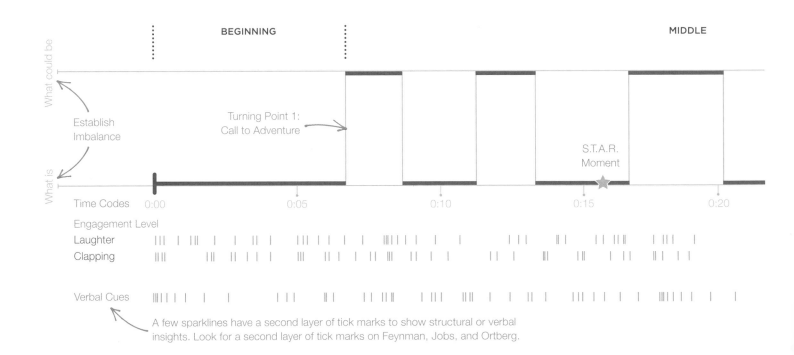

A few sparklines have a second layer of tick marks to show structural or verbal insights. Look for a second layer of tick marks on Feynman, Jobs, and Ortberg.

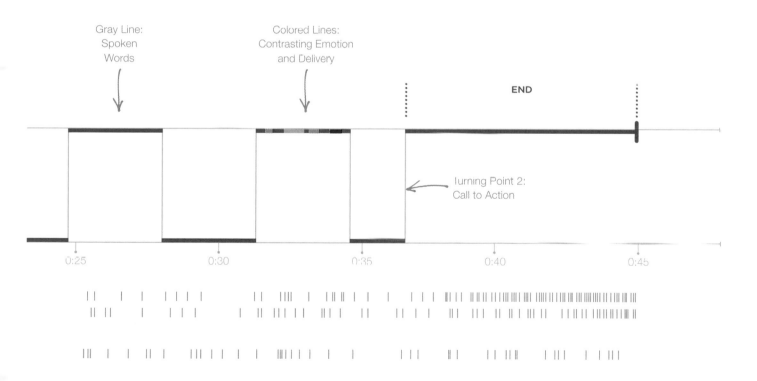

Gray Line:
Spoken
Words

Colored Lines:
Contrasting Emotion
and Delivery

END

Turning Point 2:
Call to Action

0:25   0:30   0:35   0:40   0:45

Case Study: Benjamin Zander
TED Talk

Benjamin Zander has a contagious passion for classical music. Motivational speaker and conductor of the Boston Philharmonic Orchestra, he's intent on persuading everyone to fall in love with classical music. And during his 2008 TED talk, the audience was visibly moved toward that end.

If you haven't yet seen this presentation, please watch it! Go to TED.com and search for Benjamin Zander to see this master communicator in action. WWW Less than a minute into the presentation, the audience is already responding to its content. They laugh early and often. **He energetically engrosses the audience several ways:**

- **Structural Contrast:** Zander gracefully shifts between *what is* and *what could be* by establishing a clear gap between those in the audience who already passionately love classical music and those who feel it's simply like second-hand smoke at the airport. He's determined not to leave the room until everyone is in love with classical music.

- **Delivery Contrast:** He contrasts his delivery several ways. He alternates between speaking and playing the piano. He physically involves the audience by having them sing. He moves from the stage into the audience several times, even touching the faces of the audience members! He also uses large gestures and dramatic facial expressions.

- **Emotional Contrast:** Zander tells several stories; some evoke laughter—some, tears. Though they alternate between funny and touching, each one connects the hearts of the listeners to the material and moves them (emotionally and behaviorally) toward loving classical music.

Like all great mentors, Zander gives the audience members a special tool: he teaches them how to listen to the music. They learn to identify impulses and chord progressions. He trains their ears in music theory. Many in the audience haven't loved classical music because they were unable to hear the layers of beauty within it. Zander unfolds these layers for them.

Zander brilliantly uses the music as the message as he elicits and connects with listeners' emotions. Having trained their ears to recognize the sense of longing created by an unresolved chord, he then goes straight for the heart. He asks them to remember a loved one who is no longer with them as he replays a piece by Chopin. This is the S.T.A.R. moment (page 148) in the presentation. Possibly for the first time in their lives, the audience can hear the longing in the music, and they are deeply moved.

Zander demonstrates all the components of a perfect presentation form, which is annotated on page 50.

Benjamin Zander
Conductor of the Boston Philharmonic Orchestra

Zander's Sparkline

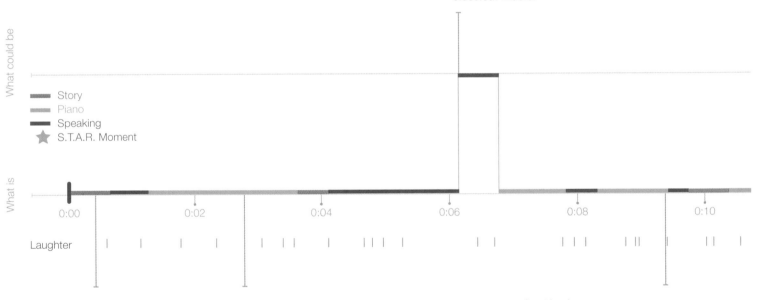

Establish *What Could Be*
Zander is passionate about showing the audience how to love classical music. He says, "It doesn't work for me to [have] a wide gulf between those who understand, love, and are passionate about classical music, and those who have no relationship to it at all...I'm not going to go until every single person in this room...come[s] to love and understand classical music."

Story
Piano
Speaking
★ S.T.A.R. Moment

What could be

What is

0:00   0:02   0:04   0:06   0:08   0:10

Laughter

Establish *What Is*
After hooking the audience with a story, Zander states, "There are some people who think that classical music is dying."

Teach Them to Listen
Zander teaches the audience how to listen for "impulses" in the music and challenges the audience to listen for them in his playing. He educates them about music theory and performance.

Engage by Singing
When he describes the Chopin prelude, he plays descending notes of a scale—B, A, G, F#—then withholds the last note (E) and invites the audience to sing it. They're reluctant at first, so he repeats his request. When the audience sings the final note, he remarks, "Oh, the TED choir!" eliciting laughter.

Emotional Contrast

Zander taught the audience how a chord pulls the music toward the home key like a magnet. As the music moves away from home into other chords, the music feels persistently unresolved. As the music persists in long, unresolved chords, it creates a sense of longing until it finally comes back to the home key. The music wants to resolve and go home. Then he says, "Would you think of somebody who you adore who is no longer there—a beloved grandmother, a lover, somebody in your life who you love with all your heart but that person is no longer with you. Bring that person into your mind and at the same time follow the line all the way from B to E, and you'll hear everything that Chopin had to say."

This time when he plays the piece, the beauty of longing and desire that was built into the piece manifests itself in the hearts of the audience. They can feel themselves in the music. People in the audience fall in love with classical music when they can understand it emotionally.

Call to Action

Zander concludes by sharing a life-changing realization that his job is to awaken the possibility in others. "And do you know how to find out [if you succeeded]? You look at their eyes. If their eyes are shining, you know you're doing it." He challenges the audience to ask the question of themselves: "Who are we being as we go back into the world? It's not about wealth and fame and power. It's about how many shining eyes are around you."

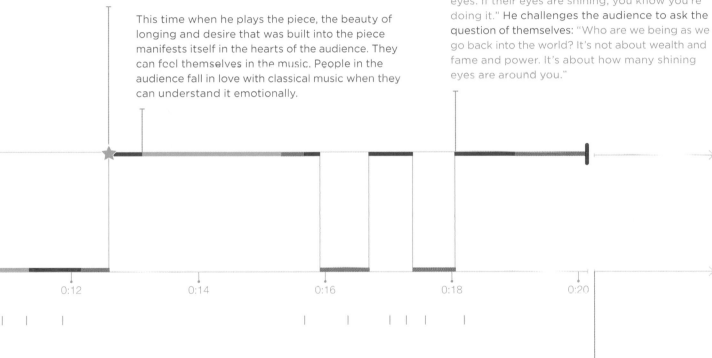

0:12   0:14   0:16   0:18   0:20

Engage by Singing

Though not shown in the video, Zander comes back for an encore in which he leads the "TED choir" in a rousing rendition of Beethoven's *Ode to Joy* in German.

Stories have been told for thousands of years in order to transfer cultural lore and values. When a great story is told, we lean forward, and our hearts race as the story unfolds. Can that same power be leveraged for a presentation? Yes.

The timeless structure of a story can contain information that persuades, entertains, and informs. Story serves as a perfect device to help an audience recall the main point and be moved to action. Once a presentation is put into a story form, it has structure, creates an imbalance the audience wants to see resolved, and identifies a clear gap that the audience can fill.

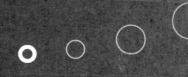

RULE #2

Incorporating story into presentations has an exponential effect on outcomes.

CHAPTER 3

Get to Know the Hero

How Do You Resonate with These Folks?

The instructions your high school speech teacher gave you to picture the audience in their underwear is now officially obsolete. Instead, you need to picture them all in colorful stockings and tunics with superhero emblems—because these are the heroes charged with carrying your big idea to fruition.

It's important to know what makes your audience tick in order to connect with them. So how do you get to know them and really understand what their lives are like? What makes them laugh? What makes them cry? What unites them? What incites them? What is it that makes them deserve to win in life? It's important to figure this out because according to the former AT&T presentation research manager, Ken Haemer, **"designing a presentation without an audience in mind is like writing a love letter and addressing it 'to whom it may concern.'"**[1] This section will help you create empathy for your audience by brainstorming the attributes of the hero and mentor archetypes.

Though your heroes might be lumped together in a room, you shouldn't view them as a homogeneous blob. **Instead of thinking about the audience as a unified clump when preparing your presentation, imagine them as a line of individuals waiting to have face-to-face conversations with you.** You want to make each person feel like you're having a personal exchange with him or her; it will help you speak in a conversational tone, which will keep them interested. People don't fall asleep during conversations (unless your conversations are boring too. If so, you need help beyond what this book provides).

An audience is a temporary assembly of individuals who, for an hour or so, share one thing in common: your presentation. They are all listening to the same message at the same moment; yet all of them are filtering it differently and gleaning their own unique insights, points of emphasis, and meaning. If you find common ground from which to communicate, their filter will more readily accept your perspective.

As an option, you might want to create a narrowly targeted message for specific people in the audience so that your presentation comes across as a personal conversation with the highest-priority individuals. Even if only one person gets it—if it's the right person—it's worth it!

You need to get to know these folks. You are their mentor. Each one has unique skills, vulnerabilities, and even a nemesis or two. The audience must be your focus while you create the content of your presentation. They are so important, in fact, that the next two sections of the book will revolve around the audience. So stop thinking about yourself and start thinking about connecting with them.

Segment the Audience

One way to get to know your audience is through a process called segmentation. By partitioning a large audience into smaller subsegments, you can **target the segment that will bring the most additional supporters.** Determine which group is most likely to adopt your perspective—the group with which you can make the greatest impact with the least effort. It's tricky to appeal to the broader audience and simultaneously connect deeply with the subset that will play a key role in helping you—but it's worth the effort.

The most commonly used segmentation method is to segment by demographics. Most conference organizers can provide only limited information about the audience: where they work, their title, geographical location, and company. You can make some assumptions from this information, but it's limited to just that—assumptions.

When I presented to top executives from a national beer manufacturer, I needed to spend time thinking about how to connect with them, because based on demographics alone, we did not have much in common in this arena. I'm a middle-aged female who drinks fruity cocktails because I imagine beer might taste like fizzy pee. That's a pretty big gap.

I didn't receive enough information from the event organizers to feel like I really knew what's important to them.

	BEER EXECUTIVES	NANCY DUARTE
Gender	34 Males, 14 Females	Female
Job Title	Executives with titles like director, vice president, and CMO	Entrepreneur and CEO
Geography	They flew in from 11 countries	I drove 3.6 miles up the road

Collecting their gender and country of origin isn't enough information to communicate with them meaningfully. Audiences aren't moved solely because they are old or young, from Kansas or from California. Their demographics are only part of the story.

Truly communicating effectively takes research. That can mean sending out your own survey that will help you gain insights or—if you're targeting a broader industry group—going online and finding popular blogs by industry icons to see what's on their minds. You might take note of what they chat about on social media sites until you reach a point where you feel you know them personally.

Don't segment the audience in a clichéd or generalized way. Defining your audience too broadly can make you seem impersonal or unprepared. It can cause your audience to feel like a statistic, or like they are being narrowly stereotyped, which can be offensive. The main idea is

that you need to define the audience in a way that's accurate and appropriate for the kind of presentation you will deliver.

Several things helped me prepare for the presentation to the beer executives. I bought subscriptions to a couple of key marketing publications to see what was being said about their brands, solicited feedback from my social network, searched for articles about them, reviewed the conversations in the top beer blogs, found their own presentations on the Web, read their press releases, and read their company's latest annual report.

The research helped me understand their challenges. Even though I only used a portion of the insights in the actual presentation, I felt like I knew them and had empathy for what was on their minds. Those insights helped me feel connected to them.

I even hosted a beer tasting with my employees, and I actually found one I enjoyed.

Case Study: Ronald Reagan
Space Shuttle Challenger Address

President Ronald Reagan was a skilled communicator who was faced with a daunting communication situation immediately after the Space Shuttle Challenger disaster.

The shuttle's launch had already been delayed twice, and the White House was insisting that it launch before the State of the Union address, so it took off on January 28, 1986. This particular launch was widely publicized because for the first time a civilian—a teacher named Christa McAuliffe—was traveling into space. The plan was to have McAuliffe communicate to students from space. According to the *New York Times,* nearly half of America's schoolchildren aged nine to thirteen watched the event live in their classrooms.[2] After a short seventy-three seconds into flight, the world was stunned when the shuttle burst into flames, killing all seven crew members on board.

President Ronald Reagan canceled his scheduled State of the Union address that evening and instead addressed the nation's grief. In *Great Speeches for Better Speaking,* author Michael E. Eidenmuller describes the situation: "In addressing the American people on an event of national scope, Reagan would play the role of national eulogist. In that role, he would need to imbue the event with life-affirming meaning, praise the deceased, and manage a gamut of emotions accompanying this unforeseen and yet unaccounted-for disaster. As national eulogist, Reagan would have to offer redemptive hope to his audiences, and particularly to those most directly affected by the disaster. But Reagan would have to be more than just a eulogist. He would also have to be a U.S. president and carry it all with due presidential dignity befitting the office as well as the subject matter."[3]

President Reagan's ability to credibly move in and out of different roles for different audience segments was a large part of what made him The Great Communicator.

The speech succeeded in meeting the emotional requirements of its various audiences by carefully addressing each segment. The circumstances gave a natural situational segmentation; it would not have been appropriate for him to address them based on conventional distinctions of gender or political parties.

Audience Segmentation

Collective Mourners	Families of the Fallen	School-children	Soviet Union	NASA

Reagan took care to connect all subaudiences to the larger audience of collective mourners. He brought disparate groups together by treating them as a single organic whole: A nation of people called to a place of national sorrow and remembrance. Eidenmuller says, "Catastrophic events do provide the basis for rhetorical situations. Despair, anxiety, fear, anger, and the loss of meaning and purpose are powerful psycho-spiritual forces that deeply affect us all. It has been said that 'without hope the people perish.' And without hearing powerful and timely words of encouragement, the people may never find cause for hope."[4]

The speech lasted only four short minutes. The pages that follow show how carefully and beautifully President Reagan addressed the various audiences that evening.

Ronald Reagan
Fortieth President of the United States

Many insights from this analysis are from Michael E. Eidenmuller's book *Great Speeches for Better Speaking*. The text in italics denotes direct quotes from his work.[5] www

Speech

Ladies and gentlemen, I'd planned to speak to you tonight to report on the State of the Union, but the events of earlier today have led me to change those plans. Today is a day for mourning and remembering. Nancy and I are pained to the core by the tragedy of the Shuttle Challenger. We know we share this pain with all of the people of our country. This is truly a national loss.

Nineteen years ago, almost to the day, we lost three astronauts in a terrible accident on the ground. But we've never lost an astronaut in flight. We've never had a tragedy like this. And perhaps we've forgotten the courage it took for the crew of the shuttle. But they, the Challenger Seven, were aware of the dangers, but overcame them and did their jobs brilliantly. We mourn seven heroes: Michael Smith, Dick Scobee, Judith Resnik, Ronald McNair, Ellison Onizuka, Gregory Jarvis, and Christa McAuliffe. We mourn their loss as a nation together.

For the families of the seven, we cannot bear, as you do, the full impact of this tragedy. But we feel the loss, and we're thinking about you so very much. Your loved ones were daring and brave, and they had that special grace, that special spirit that says, "Give me a challenge, and I'll meet it with joy." They had a hunger to explore the universe and discover its truths. They wished to serve, and they did. They served all of us.

We've grown used to wonders in this century. It's hard to dazzle us. But for twenty-five years the United States space program has been doing just that. We've grown used to the idea of space, and perhaps we forget that we've only just begun. We're still pioneers. They, the members of the Challenger crew, were pioneers.

Analysis

The State of the Union address is an annual, constitutionally sanctioned speech delivered like a national progress report—and is a significant task to reschedule. *Reagan positions himself both outside the fray as one presiding over it and as one inside of it who shares its painful reality.*

Reagan positions the tragedy within a larger picture without losing the significance of the present tragedy. He names each crew member and praises them for their courage. To further manage our emotions, Reagan again calls us to national mourning, and establishes the primary audience as the collective mourners.

Reagan narrows his focus to the first and most affected subaudience: the families of the fallen. He acknowledges the inappropriateness of suggesting how they should feel and offers praise they can take hold of with words like "daring," "brave," "special grace," and "special spirit."

Reagan then draws attention back to the general audience's interest in the larger scientific story. He then envisions the crew's place in history as transcending science altogether by calling them pioneers. *The term "pioneer" cloaks them in a mythical covering, one dating back to our nation's earliest ventures.*

Speech

And I want to say something to the schoolchildren of America who were watching the live coverage of the shuttle's takeoff. I know it's hard to understand, but sometimes painful things like this happen. It's all part of the process of exploration and discovery. It's all part of taking a chance and expanding man's horizons. The future doesn't belong to the fainthearted; it belongs to the brave. The Challenger crew was pulling us into the future, and we'll continue to follow them.

I've always had great faith in and respect for our space program. And what happened today does nothing to diminish it. We don't hide our space program. We don't keep secrets and cover things up. We do it all up front and in public. That's the way freedom is, and we wouldn't change it for a minute.

We'll continue our quest in space. There will be more shuttle flights and more shuttle crews and, yes, more volunteers, more civilians, more teachers in space. Nothing ends here; our hopes and our journeys continue.

I want to add that I wish I could talk to every man and woman who works for NASA or who worked on this mission and tell them, "Your dedication and professionalism have moved and impressed us for decades. And we know of your anguish. We share it."

There's a coincidence today. On this day 390 years ago, the great explorer Sir Francis Drake died aboard ship off the coast of Panama. In his lifetime the great frontiers were the oceans, and a historian later said, "He lived by the sea, died on it, and was buried in it." Well, today we can say of the Challenger crew, "Their dedication was, like Drake's, complete."

The crew of the Space Shuttle Challenger honored us by the manner in which they lived their lives. We will never forget them, nor the last time we saw them, this morning, as they prepared for their journey and waved goodbye and "slipped the surly bonds of earth" to "touch the face of God." Thank you.

Analysis

Reagan's next subaudience is the schoolchildren—an estimated five million—among whom are the students of Christa McAuliffe's class and school. *Reagan momentarily adopts the tone of an empathizing parent, which is tough to do while remaining "presidential," but Reagan carries it well.*

Here, Reagan the national eulogist hands off to Reagan the U.S. president. This passage contains the only political statement in the address and is targeted at the Soviet Union. He attacks the secrecy surrounding their failures, which had irked American scientists who knew that shared knowledge was the best way to ensure the stability and safety of space programs.

In this direct address to NASA, Reagan gives needed encouragement, and then turns back again to connect to the whole audience by saying, "We share it."

In closing, Reagan creates an eloquent and poetic moment. It captures the mythological sentiment surrounding humanity's unending quest to solve the mysteries of the unknown. The phrase "touch the face of God" was taken from a poem entitled "High Flight," written by John Magee, an American aviator in WWII. Magee was inspired to write the poem while climbing to thirty-three thousand feet in his Spitfire. It remains in the Library of Congress today.

Meet the Hero

It helps to split an audience into segments—but humans are more complex than that. In order to connect personally, you have to bond with what makes people human. Take time to analyze their lives, and valuable insights will appear. **After all, it's tough to influence people you don't know.**

At the beginning of a movie, the hero's likability is established. The same applies to a presentation. Successful Hollywood screenwriter Blake Snyder coined the phrase "save the cat" to describe a hero's likability. Snyder says that a "save the cat" scene is "where we meet the hero and he or she does something—like saving a cat—that defines who he is and makes the audience like him."[6] By answering the questions on the right, you'll uncover what makes your hero likable.

Liking your audience members is the first step in being genuine with them. Study them. What would a walk in their shoes be like? What keeps them up at night? What are they called to do that will make a difference on this earth? Imagine their lives by the day, hour, and minute.

Remember, because they are human, their lives are messy. They might have a sick child at home, might not have slept well on the hotel pillow, might not be making ends meet financially, or just might not feel on top of their game. Look for insights into how your idea will alleviate pressure on them if they take action.

It's easy to focus on what they do for their career; these questions help you think about *who they are.* Knowing their titles isn't enough. Let's say you'll be speaking at a Human Resources event and the bulk of attendees are directors of human resources. Go online and figure out how much money they make. Is it enough to get by based on where they live? How do you imagine they would spend their paychecks? What are the typical temperaments of people in their role? Are they spontaneous or methodical?

Keep answering the questions until you move away from what your audience members do for a job and begin to acquaint yourself with who they are as people. You can imagine their childhood. What games did they play? What was home life like? What TV shows shaped their psyche? Anything that will generate a connection.

Your goal is to figure out what your audience cares about and link it to your idea.

Who They Are

LIFESTYLE
What's likable and special about them? What does a walk in their shoes look like? Where do they hang out (in life and on the Web)? What's their lifestyle like?

KNOWLEDGE
What do they already know about your topic? What sources do they get their knowledge from? What biases do they have (good or bad)?

MOTIVATION AND DESIRE
What do they need or desire? What is lacking in their lives? What gets them out of bed and turns their crank?

VALUES
What's important to them? How do they spend their time and money? What are their priorities? What unites them or incites them?

INFLUENCE
Who or what influences their behavior? What experiences have influenced their thoughts? How do they make decisions?

RESPECT
How do they give and receive respect? What can you do to make them feel respected?

Meet the Mentor

Now that you've spent time getting into the audience's hearts and heads, it's time to look at your role as mentor. But wait—weren't you told earlier not to think about yourself? So which is it? It does seem like a contradiction, but **mentors are selfless and think of themselves in the context of others.** These exercises will help you think about yourself in terms of what you can give the audience.

Your role as mentor is to influence the hero (audience) at critical junctures of his life. The mentor's appearance in the journey is essential to moving the hero past the blockades of doubt and fear. Mentors usually have two major responsibilities: teaching and gift-giving.

In the movie *The Karate Kid* (1984), Mr. Miyagi not only teaches protégé Daniel the "tool" of karate; he gives him insights into the meaning of life:

Miyagi: What matter?
Daniel: I'm just scared. The tournament and everything.
Miyagi: You remember lesson about balance?
Daniel: Yeah.
Miyagi: Lesson not just karate only. Lesson for whole life. Whole life have a balance. Everything be better. Understand?

What insights into life can you give the audience? Draw on your own deep truths and transfer to your audience a sense for what it would be like for them to walk fully in their calling.

Stay mindful of how you fit into their lives. You are making a small appearance in your hero's grand life story to help get him unstuck and provide him with the resources to help him on his journey. Yes, you have important information to convey—maybe even a deal to close—but your presentation should offer something valuable too.

The mentor should provide the hero with important, useful, previously unknown information. You should also motivate the hero when she is fearful or hesitant and give the hero tools for her tool belt. These tools could be roadmaps for success, new communication techniques, or even insights into her soul. No matter what the tool is, **the audience should leave each presentation knowing something they didn't know before** and with the ability to apply that knowledge to help them succeed.

You mustn't come across as if the audience is helping you on your journey. You're to be a gift to them. Every once in a while, mentors gain something from the relationship for themselves, like knowledge or insights—but that shouldn't be your goal. An audience can always spot selfish motives.

Miyagi was a pretty smart dude. He got his deck sanded, car washed, plus his fence and house painted out of the deal. At times, there's benefit to the mentor, but the greater benefit should always be for the hero.

What You Give Them

GUIDANCE
What insights and knowledge will help them navigate their journey?

CONFIDENCE
How can you bolster their confidence so they aren't reluctant?

TOOLS
What tools, skills, or magical gifts do they gain from you on their journey?

Create Common Ground

Creating common ground with an audience is like clearing a pathway from their heart to yours. **By identifying and articulating shared experiences and goals, you build a path of trust so strong that they feel safe crossing to your side.** You develop credibility without coming across as arrogant. Even your magnificent qualifications should be revealed in a humble and selfless way that connects with them.

Sharing keen insights and a magical tool or two is great, but if you aren't credible, your audience won't listen. As you present, they're sizing you up: Is she articulate? Is she qualified? Do I like her? It's human nature for people to compare and validate others against their own criteria and experiences before adopting a new perspective.

Focusing on commonalities bolsters credibility, so spend time uncovering similarities. Seek out shared experiences and goals that you can bring to the foreground. A presentation that creates common ground has the potential to unite a diverse group of people toward a common purpose—people who normally might never have unified because of their great diversity. People set aside differences when they're strongly connected to achieving a common goal.

If a presentation goes badly awry, it's easy to blame the audience for misinterpretations and say, "That's not what I meant. How could they be so dumb?" In the blame game, all ten fingers should be pointed at you, not the people "misinterpreting" your presentation. You chose the words and images to convey your idea; if it didn't align with the audience's experiences, you need to own up to the misunderstanding.

I had one of those "why doesn't the audience get this obvious idea" moments when conveying our company vision in 2007. My employees are not blind; my communication was flawed. Having been through three significant economic downturns, it was easy to see the next one coming a mile away. I knew that the firm needed to make some immediate changes that would help us weather the storm. But to the team, everything seemed safe and stable. So when I delivered an urgent "danger is eminent" message, it backfired. At the end of my dramatic presentation, my employees sat stunned, feeling like I was trying to manipulate them by telling them the sky was falling. What I thought was a presentation dripping with insight and urgency, my young staff—who had only known prosperity and stability—perceived as manipulative. My message and means of communication slowed progress to a crawl. A handful understood, but getting everyone on board proved almost insurmountable. It took an entire year to reframe the issues and build momentum. Even though a downturn was coming, the idea had no traction because I didn't use symbols or experiences to which my audience could connect.

An audience chooses whether to connect to you or not. People will usually respond only if it's in their best interest. **Personal values will ultimately drive their behavior,** so ideally you should identify and align with existing values.

How You
Connect
with Them

SHARED EXPERIENCES
What from your past
do you have in common:
memories, historical
events, interests?

COMMON GOALS
Where are you headed
in the future? What
types of outcomes
are mutually desired?

QUALIFICATIONS
Why are you uniquely
qualified to be their guide?
What similar journey
have you gone on with
a positive outcome?

Communicate from the Overlap

Why do you have to go through all these questions about the audience and yourself? Connecting empathetically with an audience requires developing understanding and sensitivity to their feelings and thoughts.

People come to a presentation with their own facts and emotions stored neatly in their heads and hearts. People are wired to absorb information and transform it into personal meaning that shapes their perspectives.

It's the presenter's job to know and tune into the audience's frequency. Your message should resonate with what's already inside them. As a presenter, if you send a message that is tuned to the "frequency" of their needs and desires—they will change. They might even quiver with enthusiasm and move together to create beautiful results (page 4).

When you know someone well, your common experiences create shared meaning. My husband, Mark, can say just one word that is packed with enough meaning, and I'm howling with laughter on the ground. Granted, you probably haven't been married to your audience for thirty years—but if you do your homework, they will feel like a good friend. And friends know how to persuade one another. They have a natural way of swaying each other toward their perspective.

Establishing how you're alike also clarifies how you're different. Once you've identified the overlap, you'll have a clearer understanding of what's outside the overlap that needs to be embraced by the audience.

Your objective is to find the most relevant and believable way to link your issue to your audience's top values and concerns.

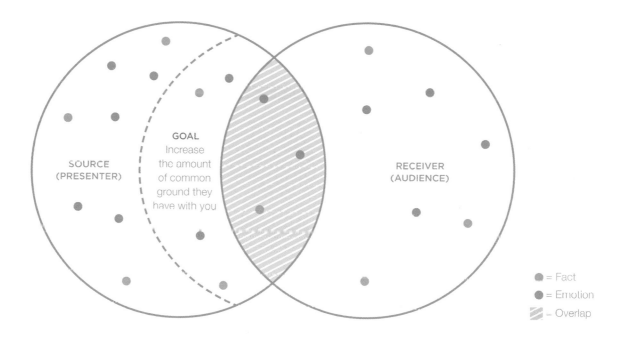

GOAL
Increase
the amount
of common
ground they
have with you

SOURCE
(PRESENTER)

RECEIVER
(AUDIENCE)

● = Fact
● = Emotion
▨ = Overlap

"If any man were to ask me what I would suppose to be the perfect style of language, I would answer, that in which a man speaking to five hundred people, of all common and various capacities, idiots or lunatics excepted, should be understood by them all, and in the same sense which the speaker intended to be understood."

Daniel Defoe[7]

When you know someone, really know them, it's easy to persuade them. Investing time into familiarizing yourself with the audience solidifies your ability to persuade.

Meet the Hero: The audience is the hero who will determine the outcome of your idea, so it's important to know them fully. Jump into the shoes of your audience and look carefully at their lives. Picture them as individuals with complex lives. Identify with their feelings, thoughts, and attitudes. Discover their lifestyles, knowledge, desires, and values. Painting a picture of who they are in their ordinary world helps you connect with them and communicate from a place of empathy.

Meet the Mentor: Embracing the stance of mentor clothes you in humility. It moves you from forcing information on "an ignorant audience" to giving them valuable tools to guide them on their journey or help them get unstuck. They should leave with valuable insights they didn't have before they met with you.

When an audience gathers, they have given you their time, which is a precious slice of their lives. It's your job to have them feel that the time they spent with you brought value to their lives.

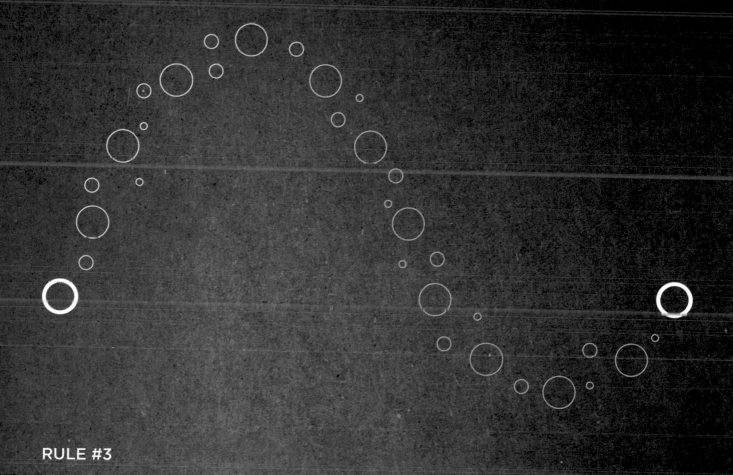

RULE #3

If a presenter knows the audience's
resonant frequency and tunes to that,
the audience will move.

CHAPTER 4

Define the Journey

Preparing for the Audience's Journey

Presentations should have a destination. If you don't map out where you want the audience to be when they leave your presentation, the audience won't get there. If a sailor wanted to travel to Hawaii, he wouldn't hop in the boat, open the sails, guess at a direction, and fully expect to arrive after a few days of sailing. It simply doesn't work that way. You have to set a course, and that means developing the right content. The destination you define can serve as a guide. **Every bit of content you share should propel the audience toward that destination.**

Keep in mind that a presentation is designed to transport the audience from one location to another. They will feel a sense of loss as they move away from their familiar world and closer to your perspective. **You are persuading the audience to let go of old beliefs or habits and adopt new ones.** When people deeply understand things from a new perspective to the point where they feel inclined to change, that change begins on the inside (heart and mind) and ends on the outside (actions and behavior). However, this typically doesn't happen without a struggle.

That struggle usually manifests as resistance—something that can be harnessed if you plan for it. When a sailboat is sailing against the wind, the sails are positioned to harness the wind. If done well, the boat sails faster than the wind itself—even though the gusts are opposing it. While you might not be able to control the severity of audience resistance, you can "adjust your sails" (message) and use it to gain momentum. When harnessed properly, the seemingly counterproductive force creates forward progress. However, just like sailing, it needs to move back and forth to get there (just like the presentation form).

The journey should be mapped out, and all related messages should propel the audience closer to the destination.

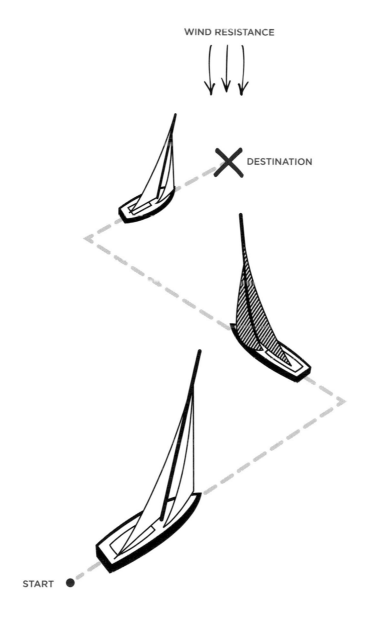

WIND RESISTANCE

DESTINATION

START

The Big Idea

A *big idea* is that one key message you want to communicate. It contains the impetus that compels the audience to set a new course with a new compass heading. Screenwriters call this the "controlling idea." It has also been called the gist, the take-away, the thesis statement, or the single unifying message.

There are three components of a big idea:

ONE **A big idea must articulate your unique point of view.** People came to hear *you* speak; since they want to know *your* perspective on the subject, you should give it to them. For example, "the fate of the oceans" is merely a topic; it's not a big idea. "Worldwide pollution is killing the ocean and us" is a big idea that has a unique point of view. The big idea doesn't have to be so unusual that no one has ever heard of it before. It just needs to be *your* point of view on the subject rather than a generalization.

TWO **A big idea must convey what's at stake.** The big idea should articulate the reason why the audience should care enough to adopt your perspective. You could say your idea is to "replenish the wetlands through new legislation." But compare that to "Without better legislation, the destruction of the wetlands will cost the Florida economy $70 billion by 2025." Conveying what's at stake helps the audience recognize the need to participate and become heroes. Without a compelling reason to move, a big idea falls flat.

THREE **A big idea must be a complete sentence.** Stating the big idea in sentence form forces it to have a noun and a verb. When asked the question "What's your presentation about?" most people respond with something like "It's the third-quarter update" or "It's about new software." These are not big ideas. A big idea has to be a complete sentence: "This software will make your team more productive and generate a million dollars in revenue over two years." It's even better if the word "you" is used in the sentence; that ensures that it's written to someone.

Emotion is another important component to the big idea. Boiling down all of the various emotions simplifies this task. Ultimately, there are only two emotions—pleasure and pain. A truly persuasive presentation plays on those emotions to do one of the following:

- Raise the likelihood of pain and lower the likelihood of pleasure if they reject the big idea.

- Raise the likelihood of pleasure and lower the likelihood of pain if they accept the big idea.[1]

For example, a business presentation that centers on "We are losing our competitive advantage" as its big idea has nothing at stake. In contrast, the message "If we don't regain our competitive advantage, your jobs are in jeopardy" makes it clear that there's plenty at stake! It appeals to employees' human instinct to survive. Humans change when there is a threat and sense of urgency. In the January 2007 issue of *Harvard Business Review,* John P. Kotter explained that "most successful change efforts begin when some individuals or groups start to look hard at a company's competitive situation, market position, technological trends, and financial performance. They then find ways to communicate this information broadly and dramatically, especially with respect to crises, potential crises, or great opportunities that are very timely."[2]

The gravity of the presentation should match the severity of the situation and accurately reflect what's at stake—no more, no less.

A Big Idea

YOUR UNIQUE POINT OF VIEW ON A TOPIC	A CLEAR STATEMENT OF WHAT'S AT STAKE FOR THOSE WHO DO OR DON'T ADOPT YOUR POINT OF VIEW	WRITTEN IN THE FORM OF A SENTENCE

THESE ARE NOT BIG IDEAS	THESE ARE BIG IDEAS
Lunar Mission	The United States should lead in space achievement because it holds the key to our future on Earth.
Client Sales Call	Our software gives your customers access to their records, which saves your employees time and increases your margins by 2 percent.
Third-Quarter Update	Third-quarter numbers are down; and to stay in the game, every department needs to support the sales initiative.

JFK knew that no one could predict the outcome of the space race, but he believed it would determine who wins the battle between freedom and tyranny.

Plan the Audience's Journey

Now that you've established the big idea and defined the destination, it's time to map out the journey. Remember, persuasion requires that you ask the audience to change in some way; and most change compels people to *move from* one way of being or doing and *move to* a new way of being or doing. Many times there's an internal, emotional change that must occur before they show signs of external change through their behavior.

Change is interesting to watch. We go to the movies or read a book to see the change that happens in the main character. This carefully planned change is called the *character arc*—the identifiable internal and external change that the hero endures.

When a screenplay is submitted for acquisition to a studio, a story analyst evaluates it by assessing the quality of the character arc. The story analyst determines the quality fairly quickly simply by looking at the first and last pages of the script. The first page sets up who the hero is when the movie begins, and the last page determines how much the hero changed during its course. This quick assessment of a screenplay determines whether the hero's journey changed her at all. If the hero didn't change enough by the last page, it'll be a boring film.[3] Great stories show growth and transformation in the characters.

In the same way a story analyst looks at the first and last page of a screenplay, you must envision and study your audience at the beginning of your presentation—and whom you want them to be when they leave. Upon entering the room, your audience holds a point of view about your topic that you want to change. You want to move them from inaction to action; you want them to leave the room holding your perspective as dear and committing to it. This won't happen without a carefully planned map.

To plan an audience journey, identify where both from and to you want to move the audience. Identify both their inward and outward transformation. If you change them on the inside, you can usually observe that through their actions. This outward change is the proof that they understood and believed the big idea. Changing beliefs changes actions.

You might be thinking, "Gosh, I'm just presenting at my staff meeting; I can skip this step." Perhaps a better option, in that case, would be writing and distributing a report. Although, if your staff meeting is about the status of a project that is over budget, you better get in there and move them from thinking being over budget is okay, to taking responsibility and working hard to ensure the budget gets back on track. This, then, is a persuasive situation that requires a clearly defined journey.

Audience Journey

MOVE FROM

MOVE FROM

MOVE TO

| MOVE FROM ONE MANNER OF BEING (INWARD CHANGE) | → | MOVE TO A NEW MANNER OF BEING |
| MOVE FROM ONE MANNER OF DOING (OUTWARD CHANGE) | → | MOVE TO A NEW MANNER OF DOING |

AUDIENCE JOURNEY FOR JFK'S LUNAR SPEECH TO CONGRESS IN 1961

MOVE FROM

MOVE TO

| Feeling the plan is too risky and impossible within the ten-year time constraint. | → | A sense of urgency because the Soviets have a head start and could remain in the lead. |
| Move from approving only a portion of the budget. | → | Move to approving entire $7 to $9 billion additional budget over next five years. |

Tools for Mapping a Journey

These pages contain a couple tools that can help trigger ideas as you map out the audience journey.

Below is a list of words culled from various articles on change management. It's not an exhaustive list of every type of change, but it can help spark ideas for how you want your audience to be transformed.

MOVE FROM →	MOVE TO	MOVE FROM →	MOVE TO	MOVE FROM →	MOVE TO
Abstain	Try	Disengage	Engage	Misunderstand	Understand
Accuse	Defend	Dislike	Like	Naysayer	Advocate
Apathy	Interest	Disregard	Examine	Nemesis	Ally
Aware	Buy	Dissuade	Persuade	Obligated	Passionate
Cancel	Implement	Divide	Unite	Passivist	Activist
Chaos	Structure	Doubt	Believe	Pessimistic	Optimistic
Close-minded	Open-minded	Exclude	Include	Reject	Accept
Complicate	Simplify	Exhaust	Invigorate	Resist	Yield
Conceal	Familiarize	Forget	Remember	Retreat	Pursue
Confused	Clear	Hesitant	Willing	Risky	Secure
Control	Empower	Hinder	Facilitate	Sabotage	Promote
Deconstruct	Establish	Ignorant	Learn	Skeptical	Hopeful
Delay	Do	Ignore	Respond	Standardize	Differentiate
Despise	Desire	Impotence	Influence	Stay Put	Begin
Destroy	Create	Improvise	Plan	Think	Know
Disagree	Agree	Individual	Collaborator	Unclear	Clear
Disapprove	Recommend	Invalidate	Validate	Uncomfortable	Comfortable
Disband	Assemble	Irresponsible	Responsible	Undermine	Support
Discontent	Content	Keep Quiet	Report		
Discourage	Encourage	Maintain	Change		

Determine Where They Need to Move to in a Process

Many presentations occur to move an audience from being stuck on a project to being unstuck. Projects and processes reach critical junctures where the team needs encouragement and prodding or the project could miss the deadline or stagnate. Another way to determine the journey is to assess the process and determine what phase they should be in (or are stuck in) and prepare your messages to move them from the current phase to the next phase. For example, you might want to move a client along to the next step in the sales cycle, which means you might need to move them from interest to evaluating your product. The graphic to the right lists common processes. The graphic below shows a master idea life cycle that you can use to get your idea unstuck.

Process Segmentation

Determine the phase in the process the audience needs to move to:

- **By Project Process:** Analyze, design, develop, implement, evaluate

- **By Sales Cycle Process:** Awareness, interest, desire, evaluation, action, loyalty

- **By Adoption Process:** Innovators, early adopters, majority, laggards

IDEA LIFE CYCLE

Choose where you feel the bulk of the audience is in your process. Make sure you address their concerns so they can get unstuck.

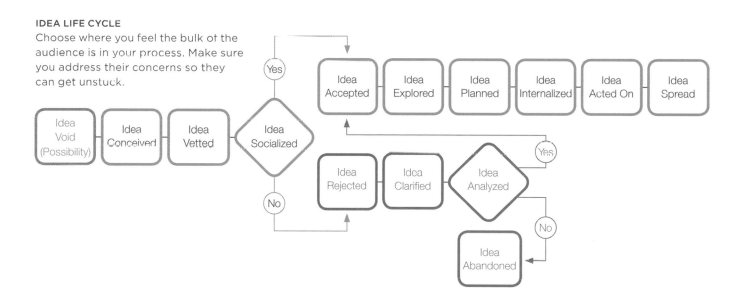

Acknowledge the Risk

People have an innate sense of fear when embarking on a journey with an unknown outcome. This unknown element is what makes change so frightening.

Change involves the addition of the new and the abandonment of the old. In order for new societies to rise, old societies must therefore fall. New technology emerges while old technology obsolesces. Even in persuasion, to accept something new means sacrificing something else.

Sacrifice is defined as the surrender or destruction of something prized or desirable for the sake of something considered as having a higher or more pressing claim. Often, our audience can't change unless a sacrifice is made. A trade-off. Letting go.

To adopt your perspective, the audience has to, at a minimum, abandon what they previously held as true. Changing their minds is like asking them to forsake an old friend who has stood by them for a long time. Losing an old friend hurts.

Even something seemingly trivial—like a forfeit of their time—might require them to risk something. Working late might mean missing volleyball practice or the chance to tuck their kids into bed at night. Be cognizant of the sacrifice the audience will make when you ask them to do something, because you're asking them to give up a small—but still irretrievable—slice of their lives. If you consider the potential risks that the audience will face when you ask them to buy into your big idea, you will be prepared to manage their apprehension and respond effectively to overcome it.

The source of audience resistance is usually related to the sacrifice they know will be required of them. Parting with their time or money is a loss to them. Your presentation is a disruption to their contented stance. You're saying they need to buy your product, be more productive, or join a movement, but they think they are fine right where they are.

Change requires a breaking down before there's a building up, and this is where the audience needs the encouragement from the mentor most of all.

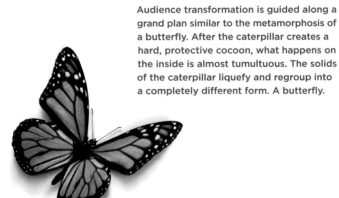

Audience transformation is guided along a grand plan similar to the metamorphosis of a butterfly. After the caterpillar creates a hard, protective cocoon, what happens on the inside is almost tumultuous. The solids of the caterpillar liquefy and regroup into a completely different form. A butterfly.

Empathize with Their Sacrifice and Risk

SACRIFICE
What would they sacrifice to adopt your idea? What beliefs or ideals will be let go? How much will it cost them in time or money?

RISK
What's the perceived risk? Are there physical or emotional risks they will need to take? How will this stretch them? Who or what might they have to confront?

Address Resistance
Refusal of the Call

There's no doubt about it; most people do not enjoy change and *will* resist. An audience might understand your plea, and even mentally accept it, but they still might not be moved to action.

In the July 2008 issue of *Harvard Business Review,* John P. Kotter and Leonard A. Schlesinger reported, "All people who are affected by change experience some emotional turmoil. Even changes that appear to be 'positive' or 'rational' involve loss and uncertainty. Nevertheless, for a number of different reasons, individuals or groups can react very differently to change—from passively resisting it, to aggressively trying to undermine it, to sincerely embracing it."[4]

Audience members will often push back or try to find errors in your presentation because if they don't, they have to either live with the contradiction between their old position and the new one you've "sold" them, or opt to change. Their resistance could be as subtle as skepticism or as destructive as a revolt, and you must deal with it squarely. How do you modify your communication to move the audience from aggressively trying to undermine your message to sincerely embracing it?

Carefully contemplate all the ways in which your audience might resist. What attitudes, fears, and limitations do they use as a tool to oppose implementing the idea? After identifying their reasons for refusal, use those concerns as inoculants. State the opposing points before they get a chance to refute your point.

An inoculation purposefully infects a person to minimize the severity of an infection. The same takes place when you empathetically address an audience's refusals by stating them openly in your talk. This will help them see that you've thought through everything—which will decrease their anxiety.

Most people don't resist simply for the sake of resistance (although some do). Most resist because you're asking them to do something that requires them to take a risk or make a sacrifice of a varying degree. For example, asking people to buy a product could make them feel as if they are risking their reputations by spending company money on a product with an unpredictable outcome.

What you perceive as resistance may be viewed completely differently in the audience members' minds. They might resist your message because, from their perspective, it puts their reputations, credibility, or honor on the line. If the audience takes this stance with your message, what you see as resistance they see as valor. They are protecting the things they hold dear and responding appropriately. Acknowledge their resistance while simultaneously assuring them that they are in good hands with you, their mentor.

Refusal of the Call

COMFORT ZONE
What's their tolerance level for change? Where is their comfort zone? How far out of it are you asking them to go?

FEAR
What keeps them up at night? What's their greatest fear? What fears are valid, and which should be dispelled?

VULNERABILITIES
In which areas are they vulnerable? Any recent changes, errors, or weaknesses?

MISUNDERSTANDING
What might they misunderstand about the message, the proposed change, or the implications? Why might they believe the change doesn't make sense for them or their organization?

OBSTACLES
What mental or practical barriers are in their way? What obstacles cause friction? What will stop them from adopting and acting on your message?

POLITICS
Where is the balance of power? Who or what has influence over them? Would your idea create a shift in power?

Make the Reward Worth It

Whether it's based on altruism or ego, people like to make a difference with their lives. That difference could be something as modest as "make this a great place to work" or as lofty as "save lives in Ethiopia."

No matter how stimulating you make your plea, an audience will not act unless you describe a reward that makes it worthwhile. The ultimate gain must be clear, whether it relates to their extended sphere of influence or possibly even all of mankind. If they are sacrificing their time, money, or opinion for your call to action, make it obvious what the payoff will be.

Rewards should appeal to physical, relational, or self-fulfillment needs:

- **Basic needs:** The human body has basic needs like food, water, shelter, and rest. When any of those are threatened, people will risk life and limb to secure them—even for someone else. People don't like to see others' basic needs go unmet, and this prompts generosity.

- **Security:** People want to feel secure and safe at home, at work, and at play. Physical, financial, or even technological security assures them that they are safe.

- **Savings:** Time and money are two precious commodities. Your presentation's reward might be saving the audience time or creating a generous return on their investment.

- **Prize:** This can be anything from a personal financial reward to gaining market share. It is the privilege of taking possession of something.

- **Recognition:** People relish being honored for their individual or collective efforts. Being seen in a new light, receiving a promotion, or gaining admission into something exclusive are all giving recognition.

- **Relationship:** People will endure a lot for the promise of community with a group of folks who make a difference. A reward can be as simple as a victory celebration with those they love.

- **Destiny:** Guiding the audience toward a lifelong dream fulfills the need to be valued. Offer the audience a chance to live up to their full potential.

In light of these categories, ask yourself the following: What is it that the audience gets in exchange for changing? What is in it for them? What do they gain by adopting your perspective or buying your product? What value does it bring to them?

As you've learned from The Hero's Journey, the hero leaves the ordinary world, enters a special world, and returns not only changed as a human being but bearing an Elixir—a reward for having taken the journey. The reward for your audience should be proportional to the sacrifice they have made.

Identify the Reward (new bliss)

BENEFIT TO THEM
How will they personally benefit from adopting your idea? What's in it for them materially or emotionally?

BENEFIT TO SPHERE
How will this help their sphere of influence such as friends, peers, students, and direct reports? How can they use it to their benefit with those they influence?

BENEFIT TO MANKIND
How will this help the humans or the planet?

Case Study: General Electric
Showing the Benefit of Change

As one of the largest organizations in the world, General Electric places tremendous value on innovation. They solve today's problems while imagining new innovations that shape the future. Admittedly, in this process, yesterday's innovations are obsolesced by tomorrow's needs. The organization is constantly in a state of flux between *what is* and *what could be.*

Communicating within this atmosphere of innovative tension isn't always easy. Chief Marketing Officer, Beth Comstock, has led a team that has navigated this territory effectively. Many of Comstock's presentations address the contrast of *what is* versus *what could be.*

Comstock coupled her contrasting words with contrasting images to amplify her message.

Comstock delivered the presentation featured on the next few pages to persuade her sales and marketing team that "growth in a downturn" is possible (notice the contrast even in her title). She wanted to move her team from the defeatist mindset of a downturn (*what is*) to believing they could innovate in a downturn (*what could be*). It's common for her presentations to address the theme of navigating through the tension of innovation.

Comstock sprinkles her communication with personal stories of risk, frailty, and victories, which makes her credible and transparent. She once even shared how previous

GE CEO Jack Welch called her only to hang up the phone midsentence. When Comstock called his assistant, she was told, "He's teaching you a lesson—that's how you come across sometimes." It was a stark lesson about leading and coaching with humor.

Comstock is a natural at communicating contrast. The setup of her presentation is below. The content has been edited on the following pages into a "move from," "move to," "benefit," and "personalized story" matrix so you can see the brilliant, underlying structure she inherently used.

Growth in a Downturn?

Jeff Immelt took over as CEO of GE in 2001 with a strategy to grow the company from within while investing more in technology/innovation, global expansion, and customer relationships. To make this happen, GE needed a stronger marketing organization to sit beside technology, sales, and the regional business leaders. For decades, GE was so confident in its products that it believed the products could practically market themselves. Then, a collective awakening occurred: Seasoned marketers could push GE to go more places, organize technologies to accomplish new feats, and help point the company in the direction of even more sales.

GE set an aggressive course in 2003 to double its marketing talent and build new capabilities. Comstock was brought on as the first CMO in decades. GE marketers established a marketing-led innovation portfolio and process across GE that creates between $2 and $3 billion a year in new revenue. Through this effort, GE defined marketing innovation as a necessary partner for technical and product

innovation. Marketers were a critical part of the team that drove 8 to 10 percent organic growth—more than double the historic rate.

But by 2008, a global economic crisis was wreaking havoc on growth rates and changing customer behavior. What happens when growth stalls? Was it time for GE to cut marketing? The decision was just the opposite. Marketing needed to be valued as a function for all seasons.

Comstock was inspired by research conducted by Harvard Business School's Ranjay Gulati. Gulati observed that companies that relentlessly focus on the customer and invest more in the pipeline in a downturn can expect to stay ahead for up to five years after recovery. Now *that* gets your attention!

GE's goal in 2008 was to stay focused on growth, no matter how tough the environment. GE needed to plant seeds so it would be poised when recovery happened. That meant investing in new opportunities and encouraging new ideas

Foster Creativity

Move to Being
Move from being uncomfortable with creativity to believing that everyone can be creative—it's frightening to move outside a comfort zone.

Move to Doing
Move from chaotic to organized through "freedom within a framework." Define the problem, make room for ideas, and work as individuals and teams.

Benefit/Outcome
Creativity takes planning in multiple iterations, but good process helps ideas stick and energizes the team.

Personalize
A team of nuclear scientists went behind the scenes at NASCAR to learn similarities in the way race cars and nuclear plants are serviced. For me, keeping an idea journal is a helpful way to create a "space" to ideate.

Navigate Ambiguity

Move to Being
Move from being paralyzed by not knowing all the answers to accepting that you will never know all the answers.

Move to Doing
Move from fear of starting to picking a path, knowing that where you end up could be very different than where you started.

Benefit/Outcome
Removing ambiguity helps you face reality, make the tough calls, and be flexible with new approaches.

Personalize
Jack Welch taught me the importance of wallowing. Having spent many years in fast-paced news environments, Jack taught me how to get to know ideas and people.

Take Risks

Move to Being
Move from being afraid of instigating ideas to fighting for a better way. Instigators are rarely welcomed but are critical to the creative process.

Move to Doing
Move from low visibility to moving forward without the answers. Ideas need a champion to turn them into action, so executive buy-in is critical.

Benefit/Outcome
If you do not jump in, you will regret the missed opportunity. When you fail fast, you fail small.

Personalize
I needed to overcome my reserve. Sometimes I look back to when I was reluctant even when I knew I could add value, then regret the missed opportunity. Now I tell myself, "You don't want to miss this. Get in there."

Develop New World Skills

Move to Being

Move from being a technophobe to seeing that in a networked world, value comes from who you are connected to.

Move to Doing

Move from the illusion of control to inviting others to join with you. Your best selling machine can be validation from customers in your network.

Benefit/Outcome

Transform your sphere of influence and turn your network into an asset that predicts future actions, needs, and solutions.

Personalize

The Obama campaign understood the power of a decentralized network of people who shared a passion for change in the political systems. They were given access to key tools, information, and the freedom to use them.

Empower Teams

Move to Being

Move from going it alone to forming partnerships, because teams with multiple points of view create diverse solutions.

Move to Doing

Move from fear of criticism to recognizing tension as an important part of the creative process. Give critics a voice, and they'll become advocates.

Benefit/Outcome

Partnerships allow you to share risk, fill in capability gaps, and focus expertise.

Personalize

I believed I had to do it all myself and didn't ask for help. I learned that you have to invite others in and that it's okay to admit you need help. People want to help and be part of something bigger than themselves.

Unleash Your Passion

Move to Being

Move from lacking passion to encouraging passion—yours and theirs. Lack of passion stalls ideas so start and end with passion.

Move to Doing

Move from personal passion to shared passion blended with compassion—it creates an energy that propels projects and meets needs.

Benefit/Outcome

You create an energy that builds on itself, that creates momentum and engagement from others.

Personalize

I've learned that sometimes my passion can overwhelm others, especially if it borders on aggressiveness. I've had to let ideas germinate and encourage others to add to them and make them their own.

Most audience members are comfortable with the view from their own perspective and don't like to admit there might be another valid perspective out there. When you propose your idea, it forces them to make a decision to either adopt your idea or live with the consequence of refusing to adopt your idea.

To ensure your idea is adopted, it's important to have a plan—a definitive destination. Determining the destination involves creating a big idea (with the stakes articulated). You also need to plan out the audience journey of where you want them to move from and where you want them to move to.

They will possibly (okay, most definitely) initially react to your proposed change with resistance. Address the resistance and risks involved so their fears are pacified and they are willing to jump in.

Make sure the benefit is clear to them. You're persuading them to change, and there has to be something in it for them, their organization, or mankind to make it worthwhile.

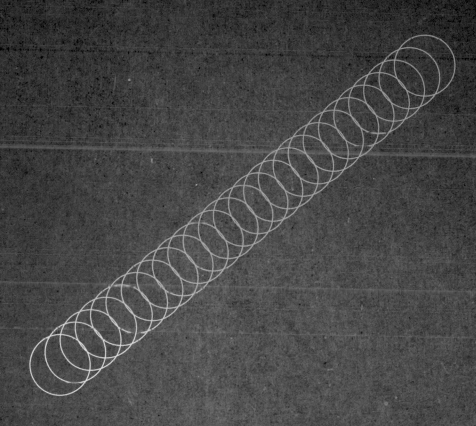

RULE #4

Every audience will persist in a state of rest unless compelled to change.

CHAPTER 5

Create Meaningful Content

Everything and the Kitchen Sink

It's now time to collect and create information. Resist the temptation during this initial phase to sit down with presentation software; it's not quite time for that yet.

This chapter covers various idea-generation techniques. It's rare that the first, most obvious idea generated is the best one. Tenaciously generate ideas along a theme until you've exhausted all possibilities. Usually, the truly clever ideas appear in the third or fourth round of idea generation.

You will use divergent thinking—the mental process that allows idea creation to move in any direction you can imagine. Divergent thinking enables new, original content to emerge. This is a messy phase, so suspend neatness and allow yourself to stay unstructured— you'll be scouting for new ideas and mining existing ones. Broadening the amount of possibilities creates unexpected outcomes, so explore every solution and suspend judgment.

Generate as Many Ideas as Possible:

- **Idea collection:** While you can avoid starting from scratch by collecting presentations from peers, that's not the only type of information out there; and regurgitating someone else's slides is not the best way to connect with your audience. Collect readily available ideas—but more importantly, purposefully mine for inspiration from all other relevant resources.

  When panning for gold, prospectors scoop up a pan full of dirt and swish it around until the heavier and more valuable gold settles to the bottom— never knowing which pan full of dirt will yield a great nugget. So scoop "dirt" from everywhere during the idea-collection phase. Look at industry studies, competitor insights, news articles, partner programs, surveys—*everything*. Go both wide and deep. Gather as much as possible about the competitor's messages so you can position yourself differently than they do. Find out everything about the subject, and roam into tangential topics for insights.

- **Idea creation:** Inventing new ideas is a different process from mining existing ones. This is where you need to think instinctively—from your gut. Be curious, take risks, be persistent, and let your intuition guide you. Draw from your creative side to generate ideas that have never existed or been associated with your big idea before. Recognize that when probing into what's possible, your ideas will exist in a bit of a fog— because you can only see the future dimly. Approach this in an open-minded state—one in which you'll explore the unknown. You're experimenting, risking, dreaming, and creating new possibilities.

Grab a sheet of paper or a stack of sticky notes and jot down everything you can imagine that supports your idea. The goal is to create a vast amount of ideas, and you'll be prompted to add even more over the next several pages! But don't worry; you'll filter, synthesize, and categorize all of them and craft a meaningful whole later on.

Collect and organize as many ideas as possible. Sticky notes make capturing ideas easy, and the best part is that they can be rearranged as needed.

More Than Just Facts

Now that you have begun to collect and create content, this first batch you brainstormed might be primarily comprised of facts. Facts are one type of content to collect—but they're not the only type needed to create a successful presentation. You must strike a balance between analytical and emotional content. Yes, emotional. This might not be a step with which you're comfortable, but it's an important one nonetheless.

Aristotle claimed that to persuade, one must employ three types of argument: ethical appeal *(ethos),* **emotional appeal** *(pathos),* **and logical appeal** *(logos).*[1] **Facts alone are not sufficient to persuade.** They need to be complemented with just the right balance of credibility and content that tugs at the heartstrings.

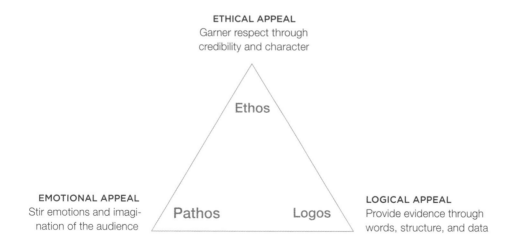

ETHICAL APPEAL
Garner respect through
credibility and character

Ethos

EMOTIONAL APPEAL
Stir emotions and imagi-
nation of the audience

Pathos   Logos

LOGICAL APPEAL
Provide evidence through
words, structure, and data

Stating fact after fact in an hour-long presentation doesn't signal to the audience *why* these facts are important. Use emotions as a tool to bring emphasis to the facts so they stand out. If you don't, you're making the audience work too hard to identify the decision they are to make. Staying flat and factual might work in a scientific report but simply won't work for the oral delivery of persuasive content.

ETHICAL APPEAL
Connect with the audience through shared values and experiences. Create the right balance of analytical and emotional appeal; this will bolster your credibility. The audience will feel connected to and have respect for your idea.

LOGICAL APPEAL
Develop a structure to keep the presentation intact and help it make sense. Make a claim and supply evidence that supports the claim. It is necessary to use logical appeal in all presentations.

EMOTIONAL APPEAL
Stimulate your audience through appeals to their feelings of pain or pleasure. When people feel these emotions, they will throw reason out the window; people make important decisions based on emotion.

"The heart has its reasons which reason knows not of."

Blaise Pascal[2]

Randy Olson's Four Organs of Communication[3]

ANALYTICAL APPEAL

ONE THE HEAD

The head is the home for brainiacs. It's characterized by large amounts of logic and analysis. When you're trying to reason your way out of something, that's all happening in your head. Things in the head tend to be more rational, more "thought out," and thus less contradictory. "Think before you act" are the words analytic types live by.

EMOTIONAL APPEAL

Spontaneity and intuition reside down in these lower organs. They are at the opposite end of the spectrum from cerebral actions. And while they bring with them a high degree of risk (from not being well thought through), they also offer the potential for something magical.

TWO THE HEART

The heart is the home for the passionate ones. People driven by their hearts are emotional, deeply connected with their feelings, prone to sentimentality, susceptible to melodrama, and crippled by love. Sincerity comes from the region of the heart.

THREE THE GUT

The gut is home to both humor and instinct (having a gut feeling about something). You're a long way away from the head now, and, as a result, things are characterized by much less rationality. People driven by their gut are more impulsive, spontaneous, and prone to contradiction. Gut-level types say, "Just do it!" Things that reside in the gut haven't yet been processed analytically.

FOUR THE GROIN

At the bottom of our anatomical progression is the groin. Countless men and women have risked and destroyed everything in their lives out of passion. There is no logic to these organs. You are a million miles away from logic in this region, and yet the power is enormous and the dynamic universal.

Don't Be So Cerebral

People are more conditioned to generate content from their heads, because institutions encourage and reward employees who spend most of their time in their analytical region (head), so most people avoid the emotional region (heart, gut, and groin). Yet it's from this more emotional region that hunches, hypotheses, and passions are generated—big ideas need those too.

Whatever your natural communication tendency is, you need to learn skills in the other regions to appeal to a broad audience. If you speak solely from the analytical region, move a bit lower; many decisions are made from emotion. In fact, your next investor might make financial decisions by following his heart. But if you communicate only from the emotional region, an analytical driven audience won't buy into your lack of proof, which could ruin your credibility.

What is it like to create presentations from your whole self—both analytical and emotional?

Ideas generated from lower regions are more innovative; they're bolder and riskier, but also more interesting. Abandon the spreadsheets and matrices and imagine *what could be*. Let your lower regions guide idea generation, and venture into more exciting adventures. Imagine the unknown without feeling silly about it. After you've exhausted these yet-unfamiliar places, turn to your head to analyze them. Make an intentional attempt to move back and forth from the head to the gut to ensure that you're using integrative thinking.[4]

"Emotions and beliefs are masters, reason their servant. Ignore emotion, and reason slumbers; trigger emotion, and reason comes rushing to help."

Henry M. Boettinger[5]

Contrast Creates Contour

People are naturally attracted to opposites, so presentations should draw from this attraction to create interest. **Communicating an idea juxtaposed with its polar opposite creates energy. Moving back and forth between the contradictory poles encourages full engagement from the audience.**

Taking a strong and clear position opens up the opportunity for others to come up with a compelling counterposition, creating contrast. For each claim you make, the odds are high that there is a polar opposite claim that someone in the room supports. Of course, you believe that your perspective is the correct one—yet others in the room will likely differ.

The gap between *what is* and *what could be* is established through creating contrast. Most people jump right to describing what the world looks like today (or historically) versus what it could be tomorrow. That's the most obvious type of contrast. But it could also be "what the customer is like without your product" versus "what the customer could be with your product." Or "what the world looks like from an alternate point of view" versus "what the world looks like from your point of view." Basically, the gap is any type of contrast between where the audience currently is and where they could be once they know your perspective.

Addressing alternate points of view and contrasting perspectives is not only thorough; it's interesting—and there's proof.

In a 1986 article in the *American Journal of Sociology,* John Heritage and David Greatbatch analyzed 476 political speeches in Britain and studied what preceded the applause. They wanted to figure out, for example, why a speech could be received in total silence, whereas other speeches were applauded nearly twice per minute. What was it that appealed to the audience enough to evoke the physical response of clapping? After studying over nineteen thousand sentences, half of the bursts of applause could be attributed to a moment in the speech where a form of contrast was communicated. The role that contrast plays in generating a response from the audience was quite evident.[6]

The exercise on the next page will help you broaden your own perspective and create room for you to consider and address the audience's alternate beliefs. Confronting their perspective gives you credibility; you'll even hear opponents say things like, "Wow, that was thoroughly thought-out."

Create Contrast

Review the ideas you've brainstormed so far. Each one of those ideas should have a contrasting idea inherent to it. There is an intelligent counterargument to each point you make. It's important to explore them all. You might not use them, but as part of your preparation, you should know what they are.

To the right is a list of contrasting elements to serve as a springboard. Most of your ideas possibly fall in one column or another. Look at all the elements in the list and generate new ideas you might not have considered. Create opposing ideas for each point that you can think of. Do this exercise for the items in each column and then repeat the process in the reverse order, which could trigger more ideas. When done, you should end up with a nice, hefty list of contrasting perspectives.

WHAT IS		WHAT COULD BE
Alternate point of view	·	Your point of view
Past/Present	·	Future
Pain	·	Gain
Problem	·	Solution
Roadblocks	·	Clear Passage
Resistance	·	Action
Impossible	·	Possible
Need	·	Fulfillment
Disadvantage	·	Advantage (Opportunity)
Information	·	Insight
Ordinary	·	Special
Question	·	Answer

Contrasting the commonplace with the lofty transforms audiences toward *what could be.* These thematic ideas are what creates the shapeliness of the up-and-down pattern in the presentation form. ⌐⎍⎍

"Recollecting our experiences and the experiences of others are precious gifts of attention that never stop gracing us with sense-giving and sense-making moments."

Terrence Gargiulo[7]

Transform Ideas Into Meaning

So far, you've generated and collected ideas. Now you'll give those ideas meaning. The structure and significance of stories transforms information from static and flat to dynamic and alive. Stories reshape information into meaning.

The brain processes information and associates meaning to it. This mental process of attaching meaning helps us categorize information, make decisions, and determine something's worth. People place value on relationships and material goods depending on the meaning they bring.

Trying to persuade by stating the features and specifications of your subject matter, product, or philosophy is meaningless—until you add a human to the mix. Take something like a medical device. The design may be lovely and the alloy strong—but the attribute that creates meaning is that it *saves lives*. Could there be a story to tell about how the device is used to save a life, or even a doctor's time? Features become valuable when they impact a human. That's where the meaning lies.

Stories help an audience visualize what you do or what you believe; they make others' hearts more pliable. Sharing experiences in the form of a story creates a shared experience and visceral connection.

The rest of this chapter focuses on how to make information meaningful and, as a result, make the audience more receptive to the ideas you are communicating.

"Stories are the currency of human relationships."

Robert McKee[8]

You undoubtedly have items in your garage that you're hanging on to that are precious to you but would be meaningless to others. I have those too.

When my Gram passed away, she had nothing in her home of seeming material value. She was a smart, quick-witted lady who'd won awards for her poetry and lived a simple life in a tiny house on an orchard. When the dreaded task of dividing up her belongings came, I knew what I wanted: one of her small stained teacups. This seemingly valueless trinket would be worthless at a yard sale, yet it was precious to me. Not because of the craftsmanship or design but because of how and when it was used. I could visit Gram for hours, sipping from that cup as she told stories. The resale value of the teacup is less than a nickel, yet at the same time, to me the value of the cup is priceless.

The value of one's belongings or even their life is not based on what it physically is; the *real* value comes from the meaningfulness associated with it by another person.

Recall Stories

Most great presentations use personal stories. As you create the content, there will be places where you want the audience to feel a specific emotion. Recalling a time when you had that very same emotion connects the audience to you in a credible and sincere way. Creating a personal catalog of stories associated with various emotions is a useful resource.

One instinctual way to recall stories is to reflect upon a timeline of your life. You can go year by year or cluster the years into phases like early childhood, elementary age, middle school, high school, college, career, parenting, grandparenting, and retirement.

However, drumming up memories based on chronology is only one way to do it. Breaking the chronological pattern can help recall a deeper—and possibly dormant—set of stories. Think about people, places, and things instead. As you explore these areas, draw sketches of what you see and jot down as many memories and emotions triggered as possible.

- **People:** You can evoke relational memories by capturing a list of the people you've known. Start by creating a hierarchical family tree that displays familial bonds. Then, begin connecting and linking relatives to each other outside of the hierarchical lines based on exchanges or situations in which they interacted in some way. List other people you've known who've influenced you and relationships you've observed: teacher/student, boss/co-worker, friend/enemy. These kinds of power dynamics make exciting stories. Think through the relational dynamics and feelings you have toward each person.

- **Places:** Carefully think about spaces where you've spent time: homes, yards, offices, neighborhoods, churches, sporting facilities, vacation sites—any place, even virtual spaces. Use your memories of these to transition into spatial recollection. Mentally move from room to room, drawing as many details as you can remember. You'll "see" things you'd forgotten. Visually moving from one space to another will trigger scenes and even long-disregarded scents and sounds. Changing gears to sketching allows you to use a different part of your body and brain, which can loosen more memories.

- **Things:** Try to catalog the material things you've possessed in your life that you deem valuable. They don't have to have been expensive items—just sentimentally significant. Why were they so precious to you? Did you love your old jalopy because you had your first kiss there? Or your old teddy bear because it comforted you when you had your tonsils out? What are the stories behind these items that make them important to you? Sketch a picture of them with as much detail as possible in the environment where they were usually found. This will trigger even more emotions and memories.

Sketching these memories is a great way to classify and recall stories. If you're uncomfortable sketching, find images to represent the stories. Create a visual trigger and jot down as much of the memory as you can—especially how you *felt* as the story unfolded. You can reference this collection of stories whenever you need to tell a personal anecdote with conviction.

When I get creatively stuck, I bounce back and forth between writing and visualizing. This process sparks new ideas, metaphors, or visual explanations.

I once needed a story for a presentation that communicated staying calm under pressure. I wanted to draw from a real childhood memory. Instead of recreating my youth chronologically through a timeline, I drew the floor plan of my childhood home to trigger visual memories. My brain traveled through each room, recalling dormant memories of my lost turtle, stage productions in the basement, and other vivid images.

But most importantly, I found my story. While drawing the floor plan of the upstairs, a memory of my four-year-old little sister, Norma, came flooding in as I sketched a closet door. She'd accidentally locked herself in the closet. The lock was made in the early 1900s and was on the inside of the closet. It had a difficult two-step process that involved turning a dial and moving a lever sequentially to open it. I felt helpless and clawed at the door from the outside while she screamed on the inside. My grandfather ran off mumbling something about finding the ax. Images of a bloody mess shot through my mind; I had to do something. I quieted Norma down enough to explain the choice of having Grandpa hack the door down or calming down and listening to my instructions. On her tiptoes, she carefully turned the knob, pressed the switch, and was freed just as Grandpa ran back into the room. I knew she could do it, but only with calm, persistent determination. The story worked perfectly!

Turn Information Into Stories

Stories strengthen presentations by adding meaning. Used well, stories, analogies, and metaphors help create significance and stimulate the senses. Stories can be one sentence long or weave through an entire presentation as a theme (page 156).

Stories are easy to repeat. Transforming information into an anecdotal format charges the information emotionally and puts it into a readily digestible format.

Below is a template that uses a shortened version of The Hero's Journey.[9] You can add as many details and descriptive flourishes with which you're comfortable, but the basic structure remains sound. Think about what types of information help illustrate your point best and turn some of that information into a story format. To the right are examples of how the template below transformed information into story.

Short Story Template[10]

BEGINNING

When	Transition	Who/What	Where
Once upon a time	there was	a manager	in marketing
In 1993	I heard about	a person (name)	in Singapore
Two months ago	I bought	a computer	on eBay
Years ago	I saw	a car	in a garage
In ten years	there will be	an event	somewhere

MIDDLE

Context	Conflict	Proposed Resolution	Complication (Optional but effective)
At the time	Which put us in conflict with	So	• What risks were there?
This was happening	We knew that couldn't continue	We tried this	• Were you worried?
	The results weren't acceptable		• What if it failed?

END

Actual Resolution	MIP (Most Important Point)
In the end ... (doesn't have to be positive)	What's the moral or core message?

		STORY ABOUT ORGANIZATIONAL CHANGE[11]	STORY ABOUT CUSTOMER INTEREST
POINT YOU WANT TO MAKE		Every cross-divisional function could benefit from a steering committee.	Midsized companies would save money if they bought this software.
BEGINNING	**When, Who, Where**	A few years ago, the sales team tackled a problem that demonstrates the cross-divisional issues I'm talking about.	Last year I met with Susan, the CEO from a company very similar to yours.
MIDDLE	**Context**	At the time, all sales groups were independent.	She was strategically wicked-smart, and, just like you, she was curious whether our software could help her business.
	Conflict	This means we were confusing the customers with many different rules, processes, and formats.	She knew that her organization wouldn't scale if she didn't have software that worked in a global environment.
	Proposed Resolution	So we decided to create a sales-steering committee.	We installed a trial version for the employees in the Dallas office only.
	Complication	You can imagine how hard it was to reach agreement on anything.	She was concerned that the employees would have a dip in productivity while learning a new program.
END	**Actual Resolution**	But we agreed to meet every two weeks to discuss common ground. Over the next year, we standardized all our processes and learned a lot from each other. The customers were much happier with our service.	Instead, employee productivity increased, and Susan received numerous e-mails about how the software will help them gain market advantage. It took her less than a week to agree to an organization-wide installation.
MOST IMPORTANT POINT		I think every cross-divisional function could benefit from a steering committee.	Your company has the same challenges and would benefit, too.

Case Study: Cisco Systems
Hop to It

Technology is meaningless until you understand how humans use it and benefit from it. This is often the conundrum in presenting technology. The emphasis is placed on the object and its features rather than on how it will help the user.

Consider the original slide to the right and the original script that accompanied the slide. Though it initially seems to describe the human component, it's really nothing more than a laundry list of capabilities.

This description is accurate, succinct, and completely devoid of charm or character. It answers the questions "what" and "how" while completely ignoring the "why." In other words, technology is capable of many things—but audiences need to be given a reason to care.

That reason to care starts with the story. Paint a picture; provide a human element to which the audience can relate; tell them "why." Once you have them hooked, you can pull back the curtain and show them how the technology really works. You will lose an audience if you jump into how a magic trick works without first performing the jaw-dropping trick itself.

The story on the following pages transforms the original presentation by capturing how Cisco's technology helped a small-business man become more agile and smart in managing his business.

When your company's tagline is "the human network," telling how humans benefit from this network is important. Weaving it into a story with a real character is even better.

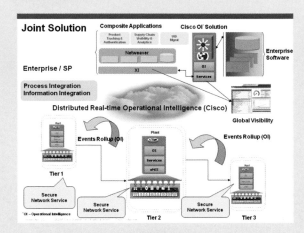

ORIGINAL SLIDE

ORIGINAL SCRIPT

"Here's an example of the power of Unified Communications in manufacturing.

The team can enter the meeting via a Cisco IP touch-screen phone or via the telephony user interface on their cell phone.

The meeting can easily move from a simple audio conference to a web conference if documents need to be shared, and also to a video conference if video content (such as a real-time view of the machinery on the line) needs to be reviewed to solve the problem."

STORY STRUCTURE

Introduce your hero early—and give your audience a reason to root for him or her.

Set up the conflict clearly, but don't reveal how the hero will overcome it—that's part of the mystery.

Provide the audience more information about the nature of the challenge; often this comes from unexpected sources or new characters.

"HOP TO IT" STORY

Dave is president of a large microbrewery. He's won more regional beer competitions than anyone else, and he's hungry for his next one, confident that his award-winning recipe will land him another victory.

Unfortunately, while gearing up to brew a batch of his new beer for the competition, he discovers his secret ingredient, his prize hops, hasn't arrived.

Just then, Dave's supply-chain manager receives a notification—the shipment of hops has been delayed in customs. The network detected the message and routed it to Dave's brewing company, where a text message alerts Dave's supply-chain manager.

STORY STRUCTURE

Develop a complication. There's nothing like raising the stakes.

Reveal a solution, but make sure it's not an easy one. This secondary challenge raises the stakes for the hero and keeps the audience on edge.

Bring the story to a head, laying out all the stakes for all the characters.

When picking up the story, recall the original premise to refresh the audience's memory.

Now Dave has big problems. His hops haven't arrived, and there's no telling how long they'll be held up in customs. He needs to launch his new brew at the competition because he's depending on the press coverage to make it a top seller this year. And he's shut down a big part of his operation in anticipation of the event, so he'll lose revenue if he can't make his deadline.

But there may be a solution: On the other side of the country, another hop supplier growing the same variety has had a bumper year and needs to unload his product before it goes bad. What will happen to Dave? Will he be able to defend his title? Will the competition organizers be able to draw the crowds they need? Will the alternate hop supplier find his customer? Find out in the exciting conclusion...

When last we left our heroes, all was not well. Fortunately, when the shipment was stopped at customs, Dave and his team were notified immediately.

Cliffhanger: It's at this point in the story you can break to explain how the technology works. The audience will be left in a state of suspense, wondering what becomes of the characters, while you provide background on the solution. This serves two purposes: You privilege your audience with information the characters don't have, and you provide the hard data you must share.

For stories with multiple characters or crises, a step-by-step approach makes the ultimate solution simple and believable.

Build to the resolution. Show the incremental steps in overcoming the challenge.

Create a climax wherein all the story threads are resolved except for one—the original challenge.

Let that resolution be the final movement, the scene that lifts the hero from one state to another.

The production manager determines the exact shortage based on the new recipe, then checks potential sources at other key suppliers through his secure network connection.

He identifies the alternate hop supplier, indicates the needed quantity, verifies the variety, and places an order.

The grower's sales rep receives the order, finds the available production supervisor, and clicks to connect to him—via multiple devices—confirming that he can ship the hops right away. The domestic supplier confirms the ship date with Dave, who is able to confirm his participation in the competition...

...which, of course, he wins again.

Hans Rosling's 2006 TED talk was the epitome of turning data into meaning. www On one axis he has female fertility rates, and the other has life expectancy. By animating the information over time, new insights emerged. The clusters of bubbles moved from the lower-right corner in 1962, where people had short lives and large families, to a completely new world in 2003, where long lives and small families are the norm.

Hans Rosling
Professor of International Health

Move from Data to Meaning

Numbers can be captivating if you move beyond just spouting the data. According to *Now You See It* author Stephen Few, "As providers of quantitative business information, it is our responsibility to do more than sift through the data and pass it on; we must help our readers gain the insight contained therein. We must design the message in a way that leads readers on a journey of discovery, making sure that what's important is clearly seen and understood. Numbers have an important story to tell. They rely on you to give them a clear and convincing voice."[12]

Numbers rarely speak for themselves. How big is a billion? How does that figure compare to others? What causes the numbers to go up or down? You can leave it up to individual interpretation, or you can explain the bumps, anomalies, and trends by accompanying them with narrative.

There are a few ways to explain the narrative in the numbers:

- **Scale:** Nowadays, we casually throw around profoundly large (and minutely small) numbers. Explain the grandness of scale by contrasting it with items of familiar size.

  WaterPartner.org's 2008 animation: "This year, 1 white girl will be kidnapped in Aruba, 4 will die in shark attacks, 79 will die of Avian flu, 965 will die in airplane crashes, 14,600 will lose their lives in armed conflict, 5,000,000 will die from water-related disease. That's a tsunami twice a month or five Hurricane Katrinas each day, or a World Trade Center disaster every four hours. Where are the headlines? Where is our outrage? Where is our humanity?" www

- **Compare:** Some numbers sound deceptively small or large until they're put into context by comparing them to numbers of similar value in a different context.

  Intel's CEO Paul Otellini's 2010 CES Presentation: "Today we have the industry's first-shipping 32-nanometer process technology. A 32-nanometer microprocessor is 5,000 times faster; its transistors are 100,000 times cheaper than the 4004 processor that we began with. With all respect to our friends in the auto industry, if their products had produced the same kind of innovation, cars today would go 470,000 miles per hour. They'd get 100,000 miles per gallon and they'd cost three cents. We believe that these advances in technology are bringing us into a new era of computing."

- **Context:** Numbers in charts go up and down or get bigger and smaller. Explaining the environmental and strategic factors that influence the changes gives the numbers meaning.

  Duarte Founder Mark Duarte's Vision Presentation: When rolling out the 2010 vision, Mark showed a graphic depicting four bold strategic moves the organization had taken every five years since its founding twenty years ago. He explained how each strategic span of five years formed the corporate values. Then, he overlaid historic revenue trends over the same five-year increments showing how Duarte weathered each economic storm, emphasizing the role each strategic surge created in growth and opportunity. There was little resistance in understanding why the next five-year plan was worth supporting.

Telling the narrative implied in the numbers helps others see the meaning of the numbers.

Murder Your Darlings

Now that you've amassed all the analytical and emotional content possible, it's time to narrow it down. Many of the ideas are unique and were possibly fascinating to uncover. But you can't say it all—and no one wants to hear it all. **The ideas need to be filtered down to the points that succinctly support your big idea.**

The pages in this chapter have walked you through divergent thinking by generating ideas. You collected factual and emotional content and considered contrasting perspectives.

Now it's time for some convergent thinking. Divergent and convergent were identified by J. P. Guilford in 1967 as two different types of thinking that occur in response to a problem. Divergent thinking generates ideas, while convergent thinking sorts and analyzes these ideas toward the best outcome.

So hopefully, all the ideas you just generated give you some great creative choices to sift through.

In his book *Change by Design,* Tim Brown says, "Convergent thinking is a practical way of deciding among existing alternatives. Think of a funnel, where the flared opening represents a broad set of initial possibilities and the small spout represents the narrowly convergent solution."[13]

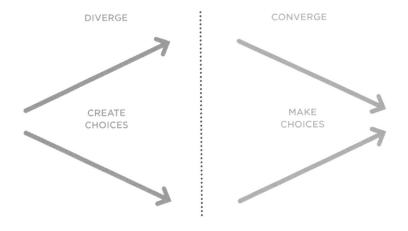

DIVERGE

CONVERGE

CREATE
CHOICES

MAKE
CHOICES

"In the divergent phase, new options emerge. In the convergent phase, it is just the reverse: Now it's time to eliminate options and make choices. It can be painful to let a once-promising idea fall away."

Tim Brown[14]

Although you may feel that all the ideas you generated are insightfully riveting and took a ton of time to generate, they need to be sorted and organized—and some ideas need to be killed off. Killed? Yes; and the best filtering device you have is your big idea itself. Review it again, and eliminate all the fodder you captured that doesn't distinctly support that one big idea.

It's a violent creative process to construct ideas, destroy them, group them, regroup them, select them, reject them, rethink them, and modify them. Use both divergent and convergent thinking processes repeatedly until you have the most salient content to support your big idea.

When you feel that you have firmly established your position and filtered your ideas, review page 105 and validate that you retained enough interesting contrast. You don't want contrast to hit the cutting-room floor during the vetting process.

Filtering is very important. If you don't filter your presentation, the audience will respond negatively—because you're making them work too hard to discern the most important pieces. While they are listening, they are determining in their minds what was interesting versus what was superfluous. And given the current social media environment, they have a forum to—very publicly—let others know their impression of your presentation. Their feedback can be brutally honest too. So if you don't edit it, the audience will be frustrated, and they might have the creative chops to distribute their thoughts to thousands of their social network followers. **Make edits on behalf of the audience; they don't want everything.** It's your job to be severe in your cuts. Let go of ideas even if you love them, for the sake of making the presentation better.

Audiences are screaming "make it clear," not "cram more in." You won't often hear an audience member say, "That presentation would have been so much better if it were longer." Striking a balance between withholding and communicating information is what separates the great presenters from the rest. The quality depends just as much on what you choose to remove as what you choose to include.

"Whenever you feel an impulse to perpetrate a piece of exceptionally fine writing, obey it—whole-heartedly—and delete it before sending your manuscript to press. **MURDER YOUR DARLINGS.**"

Sir Arthur Quiller-Couch [15]

From Ideas to Messages

Now that you've edited down the content, you're going to cluster it by topic and then turn the topics into discrete messages. Grab a fresh piece of paper or a stack of sticky notes and write out the three or so major topics that support the big idea and spread them out, giving them breathing room. The important points should be top-of-mind after all the research you've done, but if you're struggling to limit them to five, it might take a bit of mental negotiation to murder another darling or two.

Each topic should overlap as little as possible. Make sure that nothing relevant to your big idea has been overlooked. There's a thinking process commonly used at McKinsey called **MECE (Mutually Exclusive and Collectively Exhaustive):**

- **Mutually Exclusive:** Each idea should be mutually exclusive and not overlap with the others; otherwise you will confuse the audience. ("Hey, haven't we talked about the acquisition already?")

- **Collectively Exhaustive:** Don't leave anything out. If you plan to talk about your competitors, you should not mysteriously leave one out. The audience expects you to be complete.

Once you've nailed down the key topics, list three to five supporting ideas around each. To the right is an example from a presentation announcing an acquisition that would be delivered at an employee meeting.

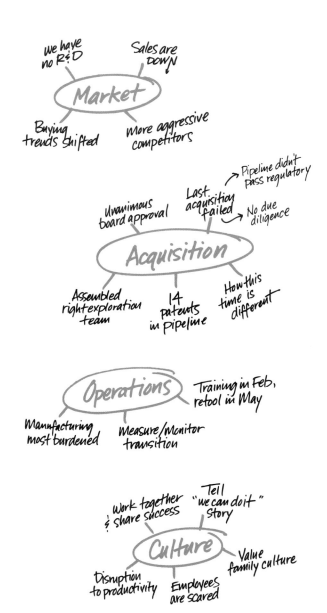

The topics you initially generate are usually a single word or a sentence fragment. In the same way that a big idea shouldn't be a topic, these little ideas need to be transformed into messages as well. Again, a message should be a full sentence that's emotionally charged. Topics are neutral; messages are charged.

Now that you've created clusters of ideas around the topics, you're going to transform the topic into a key message for each cluster.

Each message should feature as much contrast as necessary to effectively communicate the point.

In the acquisition brainstorm on the left-hand page, the first acquisition failed. They shouldn't jump right into discussing the new acquisition (*what could be*) without acknowledging the first failed acquisition (*what is*). The message of the new acquisition must include an acknowledgment of what was learned from the previous failings, or the audience will feel like this new acquisition will fail also.

Changing topics into messages ensures that the content supports one big idea and that each message has an emotional charge to it. In the next chapter, you'll be arranging and structuring these messages.

Here are examples of changing the topics on the previous page to messages:

TOPIC	MESSAGE
Market	We have an aggressive competitor grabbing market share.
Acquisition	This acquisition will be successful because we applied insights from the last one.
Operations	Operations will pay the biggest price, so let's all support them well.
Culture	Our culture is valuable and will be strengthened through this historic change.

The big idea is the well from which all supporting ideas spring, and it is also the filter to sort ideas down to the ones most applicable. Most presentations suffer from too many ideas, not too few.

Even though you explored hundreds of potential ideas and left no rock unturned, don't convey every idea, only the most potent ones.

Keep a stranglehold on the one big idea you need to convey and be relentless about building content that supports that one idea.

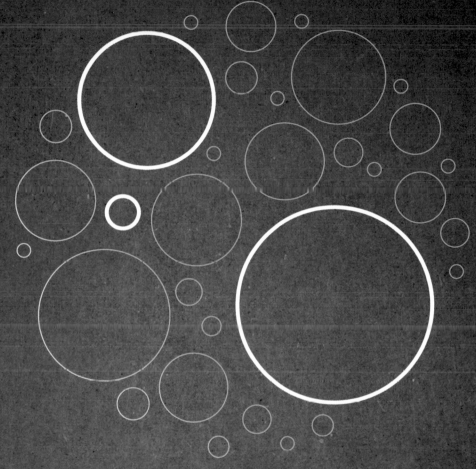

Use the big idea to filter out all frequencies other than the resonant frequency.

CHAPTER 6

Structure Reveals Insights

Establish Structure

Now that you've created meaningful messages, how do you arrange them for maximum impact? You structure them in a deliberate and logical way. A solid structure is the foundation of a coherent presentation, and shows the relationship between the parts and whole. It's similar to the couplings on a train or the string of a pearl necklace; it keeps everything connected in an orderly fashion, as if the content were destined to fit together neatly within a given framework. Without structure, ideas are easily forgotten.

"It's unwise to merely dump a pile of unstructured information into the laps of your audience. They will have the same reaction as if you take a watch apart, fling the pieces at them and say 'Here's all you need to make a watch.' You might get high marks for research and energy, but that is a low-class consolation prize. By doing this you confess that you don't know what to do with all the stuff you've dug up. Audiences expect structure."

Henry M. Boettinger[1]

Most presentation applications are linear and encourage users to create slides in a sequential order. One slide follows the other, which naturally compels the user to focus on the individual details instead of the overarching structure. To help your audience "see" the structure, move out of the linear format of the presentation application and create an environment where you can look at the content spatially.

There are several ways to do this. You can use sticky notes, tape slides on a wall, or lay them on the floor. Any method that pulls your content out of a linear presentation application will work. Moving out of a slide-creation environment helps identify holes and keeps you focused on the bigger picture. This will help move your presentation from being about a bunch of small parts to being about a single big idea.

Clustering your content helps you visually assess how much weight you've given to various portions and how many supporting points you need to get your message across. Use this technique to confirm that you're emphasizing the correct content and allocating appropriate time for each message.

Keep in mind that the structure should accommodate the audience's comprehension needs and should be assembled in a way that's palatable to them. It's natural for subject matter experts to prepare material linking ideas that are closely connected in their own minds, but remember that the audience might not see these relationships as readily. Connect your messages in a way that your audience can follow. The structure should feel natural and make common sense to them!

This section will walk you through various structural devices for organizing your presentation. Most presentations that fail do so because of structural deficiencies. When the structure works, the presentation works. If one is sound, the other will be sound. A good structure helps you work out the kinks and eliminate the extemporaneous.

Make Sense

The odds are high that you've been the victim of a meandering presentation. Unorganized presentations follow an invisible, neurotic pathway that only makes sense to the presenter. When an audience is unable to recognize structure, it's usually because the presenter either didn't have time to organize the information or didn't care enough to package the content in a way the audience could easily process.

Presentations that follow rabbit trails lead nowhere and leave the audience lost in a confused maze of dead ends.

Without structure, your ideas won't be solid. Structure strengthens your thinking. But many presentations today migrate away from the purity and clarity of structure. Don't fall for this temptation.

The most widely used structure for presentations is topical. A logic tree and outline are common forms to help visualize structure:

Notice how all the supporting information hangs off the larger topics. Points are held together under one unifying big idea from which the topics cascade down.

The chief marketing officer of a public company recently shared with me a process modification she made while developing messages for her CEO. Traditionally, she and her team would "pitch" ideas to the CEO by firing up a slide show. About three slides in, he would inevitably throw a wrench in by letting them know that this or that piece of content should be included. If he'd held onto his shorts, he would have seen that his favorite pet content was there, but he wouldn't have seen it for another fifteen minutes of slides. She laughed and said that the last time she worked with him, her team had a monumental idea. Ditch the slides and give him a substantial outline. He quickly absorbed the structure, saw his pet content immediately, and spent the bulk of the hour building on the ideas they proposed. Long live outlines!

There are benefits to looking at a presentation's structure holistically.

- It creates a snapshot of the structure so you're looking at the whole and not the parts, which keeps you focused on the construct instead of the details.

- It ensures that you have one clear big idea bolstered by supporting topics.

- It filters out tangential subtopics that may fall within the topic but that don't purely support the single big idea.

- It helps the review team get a quick read on the structure and messages, saving them time so they can give more thoughtful feedback.

TREE

OUTLINE

Big Idea

I. _____
  A. _ _ _ _ _ _ _ _
  B. _ _ _ _ _ _ _ _
  C. _ _ _ _ _ _ _ _
    1. ....
    2. ....

II. _____
  A. _ _ _ _ _ _ _ _
    1. ....
    2. ....
    3. ....
  B. _ _ _ _ _ _ _ _

Organizational Structures

There are several interesting ways to organize supporting content. Though the most common is topical, a presentation's structure can incorporate other less customary organizational patterns. These patterns can be used as the overarching structure to replace a topical one, or to arrange content within a subtopic.

These four structures have a natural storylike form that creates interest in presentations:

- **Chronological:** Arrange information related to events according to their time progression (forward or backward). This is best used if a topic is generally understood in terms of when events transpired.

- **Sequential:** Arrange information according to a process or step-by-step sequence. This is usually used in a report or to describe a project rollout.

- **Spatial:** Arrange information according to how things relate together in a physical space.

- **Climactic:** Arrange information in order of importance, usually moving from the least to most important point.

These four structures have contrast inherently built into them and work for persuasive presentations:

- **Problem-solution:** Arrange information by stating the problem and then the solution. Establishing that there's a problem helps convince people of the need for change.

- **Compare-contrast:** Arrange information according to how two or more things are different from or similar to one another. Insights surface when information is put into this context.

- **Cause-effect:** Arrange information to show the different causes and effects of various situations. This is effective when promoting action to solve a problem.

- **Advantage-disadvantage:** Arrange information into "good" or "bad" categories. This helps the audience weigh both sides of an issue.

Choose the organizational structure that makes the most sense for your message. Whichever structure you use, guide the audience through it with clear verbal or visual cues that clarify where you are and where you are taking them.

Case Study: Richard Feynman
Gravity Lecture Structure

Richard Feynman's lectures at the California Institute of Technology appealed to both the heady physics majors and non–physics majors who simply dropped in to his class for fun (an unprecedented phenomenon for a physics class). Feynman's accessible communication style earned him the title The Great Explainer.

In a BBC interview, Feynman explains how he organizes his lectures: "How should I best teach them? ...[F]rom the point of view from the history of science or the application of science? My theory is...to be chaotic and confuse it. Use every possible way of doing it. You catch this guy or that guy on different hooks as you go along. So during the time the fellow who is interested in history is being bored by the abstract mathematic...the fellow who likes the abstractions is being bored by the history. You do it so you don't bore them all, all of the time."[2]

Feynman is able to bring contrast to his lectures because he has both highly developed analytical and emotional sides. Even though he won a Nobel Prize, designed a pictorial scheme for subatomic particles, assisted in developing the atomic bomb, and predicted nanotechnology, he also regularly performed on the bongo drums. He believed his most prized asset was his insatiable curiosity instilled by his father. "My father taught me to notice things," Feynman said. "I'm always looking, like a child, for the wonders I know I'm going to find."[3] Humor and curiosity are the emotions that Feynman draws on again and again to present a fascinating—and balanced—view of science.

Feynman communicated from both his head and his heart in each lecture.

Analytical Devices:

- **Signal:** Feynman uses organizational signals to help the students understand how the structural pieces of a lecture fit together. He states the structure at the beginning and uses rhetorical questions and verbal signals when transitioning to new points.

- **Itemize:** He breaks some sections into chunks by stating how many points he is going to make and then articulating what point he will be covering as his lectures progress.

- **Visualize:** Feynman regularly used 35 mm slides, overheads, and the chalkboard, but he didn't overuse them. He used dramatic gestures and sound effects to accompany his lectures instead of blackboards covered with esoteric symbols.[4]

Emotional Devices:

- **Wonderment:** Feynman's childlike curiosity drove him toward science while also influencing his lectures with poetic phrases of wonderment, not only for science but for life. Feynman didn't just talk about physics; he marveled at the subject, and the magnificent beauty and brilliance of nature.

- **Humor:** Feynman had a self-deprecating sense of humor and a knack for weaving in humor related to the subject matter. He knew that an entertaining story is often more readily received than a well-reasoned lecture.[5] He interjected humor in almost even increments across his lectures.

The sparkline on pages 132 to 133 reflects Feynman's ability to employ the power of contrast. www

Richard Feynman
Professor, California Institute of Technology

Feynman's Sparkline

As you've learned, contrast is critical to holding an audience's attention. Feynman's lectures are a magnificent example of contrast and structure. Some academic topics simply can't contrast between *what is* and *what could be* until they lay the foundation of *what is over* several lectures.

In this lecture on the law of gravity, Feynman masterfully incorporates contrast by moving back and forth between fact

(mathematics) and context (history) in nearly perfect timing. Technically, this sparkline should be one flat *what is* line. So we'll pretend we've zoomed in on that line to look more closely at the contrast between fact and context. (See www for a visionary presentation by Feynman that does traverse between *what is* and *what could be.*)

Create a Sense of Wonderment
Feynman uses carefully crafted phrases of wonderment that express his affection for the subject: "This law has been called the greatest generalization achieved by the human mind. And you can get already, from my introduction, that I'm interested not so much in the human mind as in the marvel of nature, who can obey such an elegant and simple law as this law of gravitation. So our main concentration will not be on how clever we are to have found it all out but on how clever she is to pay attention to it!"

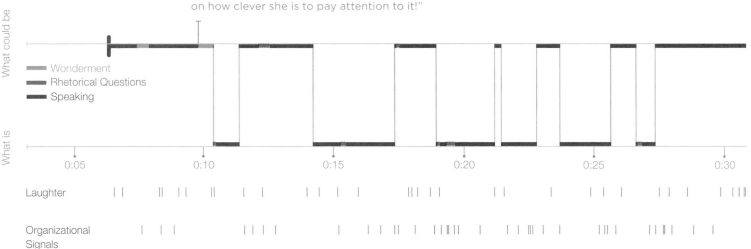

Signal the Audience
The tick marks above represent numerous signals of how the lecture was organized. He uses three types of organizational signals:[6]

Introductions
"What I want to talk to you about…" "I am going to try to give…" "Now I've chosen…" "What I'd like to do in this lecture."

New Key Points
"First,…" "Next,…" "In the meantime,…" "The next point…" "For instance,…" "Then,…" "Further,…" "In addition,…" "The next question is,…" "Another problem came up,…" "Onward!"

Conclusions
"So it became apparent…" "So an interesting proposal is made…" "But the most impressive fact is…" "Finally,…"

Create a Sense of Wonderment
"It's one of the most beautiful things in the sky—as good as sea waves and sunsets."

Make the Audience Think
Feynman sprinkles rhetorical questions as structural devices throughout his lecture like these: "Now what is this law of gravitation that we're going to talk about? The force of the moon on the earth is balanced, but by what? So something's the matter with the law?"

New Bliss
"Nature uses only the longest threads to weave her patterns so that each small piece of her fabric reveals the organization of the entire tapestry."

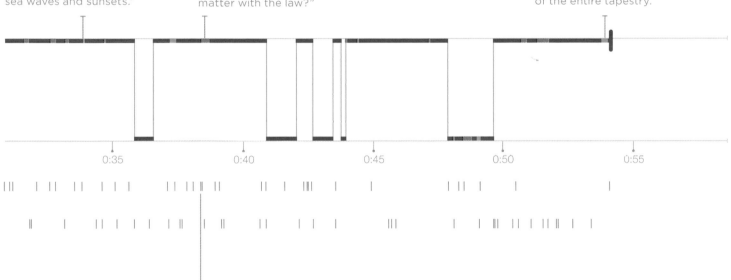

0:35   0:40   0:45   0:50   0:55

Engage with Laughter
Feynman infuses his lectures with funny commentary to keep the students engaged. He loses his place in his notes, stumbles a bit, and makes a joke at the same time: "Now that shows that gravitation extends to the great distances, but Newton said that everything attracted everything else. Do I attract you? Excuse me, I mean, do I attract you physically? I didn't mean that. What I mean is..."

Order Messages for Impact

Structure can be used to drive a desired outcome. Where and how you associate one piece of information with another creates meaning and determines how others will receive it. Skillfully arranged information creates emotional appeal and leads to the desired emotional impact at the end of the presentation.

Below is an example of a third-quarter update presentation. Most organizations regularly deliver these reports to communicate the progress being made toward corporate goals. Notice that the "move to" states that the employees should feel confident and motivated to help.

BIG IDEA	MOVE FROM		MOVE TO
Q3 revenue is down, and we're still in the lead, but if we slow down, we'll lose market share	Unsure about the company's future	→	Confident we will succeed
	Financial distractions breeding low productivity	→	Motivated to create even better products next quarter

Demotivating Structure

This structure does not motivate the audience to feel confident that they will succeed.

Sticky notes: *Revenue is down* · *# of new clients is up 15%* · *Our market share is up* · *Launching new products today* · *Doing well compared to competitors* · *We missed our Q3 forecast*

Script

Welcome, everybody, to the Q3 update. I just want to let you know that the Q3 revenue was down. The rumors are true.

The numbers are down. But hey, we're up 15 percent in number of new clients. That's good. Good job, everyone.

Our market share is also up, so that's not bad.

And you guys were able to turn out some new products this quarter, and I'm really proud of you for that.

We're not doing too bad compared to our competitors.

All this happened in a quarter in which the analysts predicted we'd be down, so it was expected. Thanks for coming today, and have a great day.

Motivating Structure

Now look at the same material presented in a different order with a pinch of added emotional appeal. Simple structural shifts and celebratory marvel changed the presentation's tone and outcome. Each point builds on the previous one, and it culminates in a motivating crescendo.

We missed our Q3 forecast	# of new clients is up 15%	Revenue is down	Doing well compared to competitors	Our market share is up	Launching new products today

Script

Welcome, everybody, to the Q3 update. When the forecasters looked at this quarter, they said our industry—our company in particular—was the little engine that couldn't. They said we wouldn't be able to make the climb.

In spite of that, we have shaken up the market in a down economy! Our new-client wins are up 15 percent over last year. In fact, four of the new clients are large multinational organizations that have been on our target list for over three years!

Yes, revenue is down, but let's give that context: The economy is down; our industry tracks with the economy, and so it's down; our company is a leader in our industry and tracks with it, so of course our revenue would be down.

But how did we do compared to our competitors? SuperCo is down 12 percent. DuperCo is down 8 percent. How far down are we? <pause> We are down only 2 percent.

So how has that impacted our market share? We have made significant gains—not only domestically but also abroad.

Even though the marketplace has endured a season of chaos and uncertainty, you have made this season one of my proudest moments.

Just look at the products we'll be rolling out in Q4. Wow, aren't they beautiful? It takes innovation and tenacity to create stunning products with this magnitude of market disruption, and you did it! If you can be this creative in an uncertain environment, I can't wait to see what you'll do when the market turns around. We're not only the engine that could; we're an engine that can't be stopped!

The way information is structured makes a difference in the outcome.

Create Emotional Contrast

Audiences enjoy it when presentations convey emotional contrast and appeal; however, most presentations lack this because it requires an additional step and can be an elusive element to include.

Involving the audience emotionally helps them form a relationship with you and your message. According to Peter Guber, "Business leaders must recognize that how the audience physically responds to the storyteller is an integral part of the story and its telling. Communal emotional response—hoots of laughter, shrieks of fear, gasps of dismay, cries of anger—is a binding force that the storyteller must learn how to orchestrate through appeals to the senses and the emotions."[7]

Moving between analytical and emotional content is another form of contrast. Remember, contrast is very important for keeping the audience interested. Switching between the two creates contrast.

Presentation Content Types

Below are two columns listing typical presentation content. Hard drives around the world are packed with slides from the left-hand section, but only a tiny percentage have slides from the right-hand section.

ANALYTICAL CONTENT		EMOTIONAL CONTENT	
Diagram	Specimen, exhibit	Biographical or fictitious stories	Shocking or scary statements
Feature	System	Benefits	Evocative images
Data	Process	Analogies, metaphors, anecdotes, parables	Invitations to marvel or wonder
Evidence	Facts	Props or dramatization	Humor
Example	Supporting documentation	Suspenseful reveals	Surprises
Case study			Offers, deals

Look at any of the analytical topics from the list on the left. They typically have no emotional charge to them—neither pain nor pleasure. Yet all could be presented in a way that transforms traditionally analytical material into emotional material. For example, a simple diagram of a small circle within a larger circle could convey that an acquisition occurred. The diagram is neutral until you tell the story of the struggle it took to acquire the company, or the heroics displayed by both parties to expedite the acquisition. Data is purely analytical until you explain *why* the ups and downs exist.

Contrast Analytical and Emotional Content

Let's review the Q3 update presentation from the previous pages once again. A typical quarterly update presentation is full of data and reportlike material that isn't likely to connect employees to the message.

Here's how the analytical information was modified in the earlier example:

We missed our Q3 forecast	# of new clients is up 15%	Revenue is down	Doing well compared to competitors	Our market share is up	Launching new products today
~~DATA~~	DATA	DATA	DATA	~~DATA~~	~~DATA~~
METAPHOR				**SLOW REVEAL**	**INVITATION TO MARVEL**
The little engine that couldn't.				Suspenseful progression and long pause.	Wonderment: "Aren't they beautiful?"

Inventory your slides and identify any content that can be transformed from analytical to emotional. Change it wherever appropriate.

In the movies, alternating emotion is called beats. Beats are the smallest structural element in a movie; there can be several in one scene. Scenes are analyzed to make sure there is a shift of emotion in each scene. Screenwriters carefully ensure that the emotions are moving between pain and pleasure so that the audience remains engaged.[8]

Moving back and forth between analytical and emotional content engages presentation audiences in the same way.

Contrast the Delivery

The chronic bombardment of media and entertainment has transformed us into an impatient culture. The entertainment industry continues to churn out new, innovative ways to engross our minds and hearts and provide us with various avenues of escape.

Audiences have become accustomed to quick action, rapid scene changes, and soundtracks that make the heart race. These advances in entertainment have set high expectations for visual and visceral stimulation and have undermined our ability to sit attentively for an hour while a speaker drones on. Most squirm within ten minutes and wish they had a remote control to flip to something more interesting.

Changing up delivery methods from traditional slide read-along to less conventional means keeps the audience interested and creates an element of surprise. Use alternate media, multiple presenters, and interaction to keep your talk alive, but be aware that these mode changes need to be carefully planned. Several can and should occur within an hour.

The key to getting and holding attention is having something new happen continually. This creates a sense that something is always "going on." Changing delivery modes can include physical movement on the stage. People feel compelled to watch visual events carefully because of our natural fight or flight instinct. Changes in media, alternating presenters, or even something as simple as a dramatic gesture creates variety for the audience and holds their interest.

Overuse of slides diminishes the power of human connection. Because genuine human connection is rare, you should capitalize on moments when you're presenting in person. An audience will deem a presentation a success if they feel they interacted with you. Lowering your dependency on slides helps facilitate this sense of connectedness.

Varying the delivery method between traditional and less traditional methods creates contrast: Below is a list of delivery methods that contrast. You can see how delivering using nontraditional methods will make the presentation more interesting.

TRADITIONAL	NONTRADITIONAL

Stage

Be the main event •	Share the main event
Hide behind podium •	Be free to roam
Use stage as-is •	Use stage as a selling

Style

Serious business tone •	Humor and enthusiasm
Confined expressiveness •	Large expressiveness
Monotone •	Vocal and pace variety

Visuals

Read slides •	Minimize slides
Static images •	Moving images
Talk about your product •	Show them your product

Interaction

Minimize disruptions •	Plan disruptions
Resist live feedback •	Embrace real-time feedback
Request silence •	Encourage exchanges

Content

Familiarity with features •	Wonderment and awe at features
Flawless knowledge •	Self-deprecating humanness
Long-winded rambles •	Memorable, headline-sized sound bites

Involvement

One-way delivery •	Polling, shout-outs, game playing, writing, drawing, sharing, singing, and question-asking

Use as many variations as possible to keep it interesting. Mix it up to create contrast!

Putting Your Story on the Silver Screen

You're finally at the last step of the presentation creation process. Now that all your messages are clear and structured, it's time to storyboard the slides.

Before opening presentation software, keep in mind the following:

One idea per slide: Each slide should have only one message. There's no reason to crowd several ideas onto one slide. Slides are free; make as many slides as you need. Give each idea its own moment on the stage. The audience visually re-engages each time you advance to the next slide, so having several well-paced slides will re-lure them visually each time you click.

Keep it simple: Sketch out small visual representations of your ideas on paper or sticky notes. Constraining your ideas to a small sketch space guides you to simple, clear words and pictures (as proof of concept) before creating them in presentation software. Even if you don't have an image, nice big type on the screen is better than dense prose.

Turn words into pictures: Turning words into pictures is easy if you understand the relationship between the words on the slide. Look at one of your bullet slides. Each piece of content has some sort of relationship with the other content because when you were assembling the slide, it "felt" like they belonged together. Circle all the verbs or nouns on the slide and think through how they are all related to each other. Odds are, the relationships they form fall into one of the categories below.

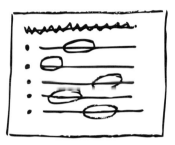

Circle either the verbs or nouns in the bullet points and determine their relationship to each other.

Various Types of Visual Relationships[9]

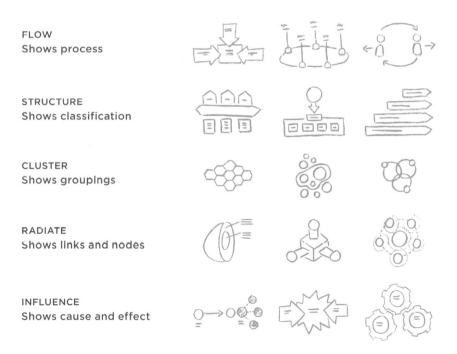

FLOW
Shows process

STRUCTURE
Shows classification

CLUSTER
Shows groupings

RADIATE
Shows links and nodes

INFLUENCE
Shows cause and effect

Note: If you want insights into how to create slides, pick up these two books: *Presentation Zen* by Garr Reynolds and *Slide:ology* by yours truly.

Process Recap

If you've been using sticky notes to collect and organize your ideas over the last two chapters, this is what the process should look like.

GENERATE IDEAS	FILTER DOWN	CLUSTER	CREATE MESSAGES	ARRANGE MESSAGES
Collect, create, and record as many ideas as possible.	Filter down to the best ideas that support your big idea.	Cluster ideas by topic.	Turn topics into charged messages in the form of a sentence.	Place messages in an order that creates the most impact.
page 98 to 117	page 118 to 119	page 120 to 121	page 120 to 121	page 126 to 134

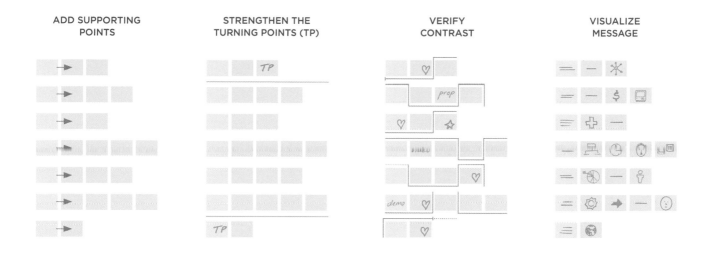

ADD SUPPORTING POINTS	STRENGTHEN THE TURNING POINTS (TP)	VERIFY CONTRAST	VISUALIZE MESSAGE
Each message needs supporting evidence in the form of slides.	Get your acts together! Ensure you have a clear beginning, middle, and end with strong turning points.	Validate the content contour, emotional contrast, and delivery contrast.	Once the message and the structure are final, turn the words into pictures.

page 128 to 129

page 38 to 39
page 42 to 45

page 46 to 47
page 136 to 137

page 140 to 141

Everything has inherent structure. A leaf, a building, and even ice cream each have a (molecular) structure. Structure drives the shape and expression of everything. The same is true for presentations. How they are structured determines how they are perceived. Changes to the structure, whether grand or small, alter the receptivity of the content.

To validate the structure, pull your presentation out of the linear slide-making environment and look at the structure spatially and holistically to ensure that it is sound, then arrange the flow for greatest impact.

Structure allows your audience to follow your thought process. If you don't have clear structure then you end up jumping around and making random connections to ideas that are unclear to the audience. Solid structure causes ideas to flow logically and helps the audience see how the points connect to each other.

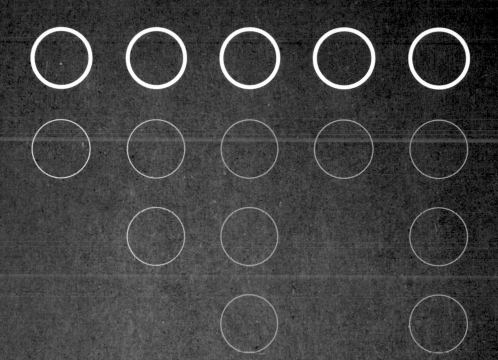

RULE #6

Structure is greater than the sum of its parts.

CHAPTER 7

Deliver Something They'll Always Remember

Create a S.T.A.R. Moment

Create a moment where you dramatically drive the big idea home by intentionally placing *Something They'll Always Remember—a S.T.A.R. moment*—in each presentation. This moment should be so profound or so dramatic that it becomes what the audience chats about at the watercooler or appears as the headline of a news article. Planting a S.T.A.R. moment in a presentation keeps the conversation going even after it's over and helps the message go viral.

Since you might be presenting to an audience that sees lots of presentations—like a venture capitalist or a customer who is reviewing several vendors—you want to stand out two weeks after you presented, when they're making their final decision. You want them to remember YOU instead of all the other presenters they encountered.

The S.T.A.R. moment should be a significant, sincere, and enlightening moment during the presentation that helps *magnify* your big idea—not distract from it.

There are five types of S.T.A.R. moments:

* **Memorable Dramatization:** Small dramatizations convey insights. They can be as simple as a prop or demo, or something more dramatic, like a reenactment or skit.

* **Repeatable Sound Bites:** Small, repeatable sound bites help feed the press with headlines, populate and energize social media channels with insights, and give employees a rally cry.

* **Evocative Visuals:** A picture really is worth a thousand words—and a thousand emotions. A compelling image can become an unforgettable emotional link to your information.

* **Emotive Storytelling:** Stories package information in a way that people remember. Attaching a great story to the big idea makes it easily repeatable beyond the presentation.

* **Shocking Statistics:** If statistics are shocking, don't gloss over them; draw attention to them.

The S.T.A.R. moment shouldn't be kitschy or cliché. Make sure it's worthwhile and appropriate, or it could end up coming off like a really bad summer camp skit. Know your audience and determine what will resonate best with them. Don't create something that's overly emotionally charged for an audience of biochemists.

S.T.A.R. moments create a hook in the audience's minds and hearts. They tend to be visual in nature and give the audience insights that supplement solely auditory information.

Famous S.T.A.R. Moments

RICHARD FEYNMAN

Richard Feynman helped investigate the space shuttle *Challenger* disaster. He quickly identified the failure of a crucial O-ring as the probable cause of the explosion. To illustrate his point, he bent and clamped a piece of the rubber O-ring and secretly placed it in a cup of ice water. At a perfectly timed moment, he loosened the clamp and as the rubber slowly uncurled he said, "...[F]or more than a few seconds, there is no resilience in this particular material when it is at a temperature of 32 degrees."[1] The press went nuts because it should have expanded in a millisecond. www

BILL GATES

Through his philanthropy, Bill Gates hopes to solve some of the world's biggest problems, including malaria. In his 2009 TED talk, Gates established the gravity of this disease by stating that millions have died, and 200 million people are suffering from it at any given time. He then stated that more money is spent developing baldness drugs on behalf of wealthy men than on fighting malaria for the poor. At that moment, he released a jar of mosquitoes into the room saying, "There's no reason only poor people should have the experience."[2] www

STEVE JOBS

Steve Jobs is a master at unveiling Apple products in intriguing ways. "This is the MacBook Air," he said in January 2008, "so thin it even fits inside one of those envelopes you see floating around the office." With that, Jobs walked to the side of the stage, picked up one such envelope, and pulled out a MacBook Air. The audience went wild as the sound of hundreds of cameras clicking and flashing filled the auditorium. "You can get a feel for how thin it is. It has a full-size keyboard and full-size display. Isn't it amazing? It's the world's thinnest notebook," said Jobs.[3]

Michael Pollan
Author of *The Omnivore's Dilemma* and *In Defense of Food*

Case Study: Michael Pollan
Memorable Dramatization

Michael Pollan is a natural storyteller who teaches people where food comes from. His books, *The Omnivore's Dilemma* and *In Defense of Food,* have reshaped how Americans think about the current food system.

When Pollan spoke at *Pop!Tech* in the fall of 2009, there was one point in particular where he wanted to leave a deep impression on the audience. He and his team had calculated how much crude oil it takes to create a fast food double cheeseburger. It was a staggering amount, and he wanted that message to stick.

When he was introduced at the beginning of his presentation, Pollan walked on stage carrying a paper bag from a fast food chain. "A little something for later," he said. He placed it on a table in the middle of the stage and started his presentation—thereby leaving the audience in suspense about the prop on the table.

Later, when Pollan was drawing connections between oil and the food supply, he said, "I want to show you how much oil goes into producing this [cheeseburger]." He pulled out the burger from the paper bag. Then he pulled out an empty eight-ounce glass and a container full of oil. He filled the glass with oil. "But that's not all. You need another eight ounces." He reached under the table and pulled out a second glass. Then he did it again. And again. In all, it took twenty-six ounces of oil to produce one double cheeseburger. www

Showing the audience the burger next to the crude oil used to produce it was a disturbing visual—one that the audience would almost certainly remember the next time they made food choices.

Repeatable Sound Bites

If people can easily recall, repeat, and transfer your message, you did a great job conveying it. To achieve this, you should have a handful of succinct, clear, and repeatable sound bites planted in your presentation that people can effortlessly remember.

A thoroughly considered sound bite can create a S.T.A.R. moment—not only for the people present in the audience but also for the ones who will encounter your presentation through broadcast or social media channels.

- **Press:** Coordinate key phrases in your talk with the same language in the press release. Repeating critical messages verbatim ensures that the press will pick up the right sound bites. The same is true for any camera crews that might be filming your presentation. Make sure you have at least a fifteen- to thirty-second message that is so salient it will be obvious to the reporter that it should be featured in the broadcast.

- **Social Media:** Create crisp messages. Picture each person in the audience as a little radio tower empowered to repeat your key concepts over and over. Some of the most innocent-looking audience members have

fifty thousand followers in their social networks. When one sound bite is sent to their followers, it can get re-sent hundreds of thousands of times.

- **Rally Cry:** Craft a small, repeatable phrase that can become the slogan and rallying cry of the masses trying to promote your idea. President Obama's campaign slogan, "Yes We Can," originated from a speech during the primary elections.

Take time to carefully craft a few messages with catchy words. For example, Neil Armstrong used the six hours and forty minutes between his moon landing and first step to craft his statement. Phrases that have historical significance or become headlines don't just magically appear in the moment; they are mindfully planned.

Once you've crafted the message, there are three ways to ensure the audience remembers it: First, repeating the phrase more than once. Second, punctuating it with a pause that gives the audience time to write down exactly what you said. And finally, projecting the words on a slide so they receive the message visually as well as orally.

BELOW ARE A FEW RHETORICAL DEVICES THAT CREATE A MEMORABLE SOUND BITE.

- **Imitate a famous phrase:** *Golden Rule:* Do unto others as you would have them do unto you.

  Imitation: Never give a presentation you wouldn't want to sit through yourself.

- **Repeat words at the beginning of a series:** "It was the best of times, it was the worst of times, it was the age of wisdom, it was the age of foolishness..."
  Charles Dickens, *A Tale of Two Cities*

- **Repeat words in the middle of a series:** "We are troubled on every side, yet not distressed; we are perplexed, but not in despair; persecuted, but not forsaken; cast down, but not destroyed..."
  Apostle Paul to the Corinthians

- **Repeat words at the end of a series:** "...and that government of the people, by the people, for the people shall not perish from the earth."
  Abraham Lincoln, Gettysburg Address

"Never in the field of human conflict was so much owed by so many to so few."

Winston Churchill

"If it doesn't fit, you must acquit."

Johnny Cochran

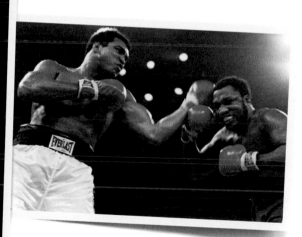

"Mr. Gorbachev, tear down this wall."

Ronald Reagan

"That's one small step for (a)* man, one giant leap for mankind."

Neil Armstrong

*When Armstrong composed this phrase, it included an "a." But the transmission dropped it and critics thought he'd botched it. Recent analysis of the recording shows evidence it was spoken and it was dropped in transmission.⁴

"I float like a butterfly and sting like a bee."

Muhammad Ali

Evocative Visuals

Images can evoke the full range of emotion, from pain to pleasure. **While using eloquent, descriptive words is one way to create an image, a photograph or illustration can frequently leave a more vivid imprint in the audience's hearts and minds.** When the human mind recalls an image, it also recalls the emotion associated with the image.

Your presentation can use one large full-screen image to convey a point, or pair images together to create conflicted emotions like the examples on the right.

Two recent occasions were publicized on an international scale through images of ink-stained fingers. In one, fingers were stained to prevent double voting. In the other, fingers were stained to tyrannically enforce voting. Each evoked very different emotions.

January 30, 2005: Iraqis voted for the first time since the fall of Saddam Hussein. Militants tried to stop the voting by setting off dozens of explosives that shook Baghdad. Proud citizens raised their purple digits (showing they had voted) as gestures of support for democracy and in defiance of terrorist threats.

June 27, 2008: After Robert Mugabe was defeated in Zimbabwe's presidential elections, he mandated a run-off ballot on which he was the only candidate and resolved to hold onto power through fraud, corruption, and intimidation. Voters in Zimbabwe were required to show their ink-stained fingers to prove they had voted. If they didn't, they could be beaten and forced to vote, and they would face severe consequences at the hands of government agents.

It's effective to recall real events like the stories above, but using images often conveys emotional force that words cannot match—particularly when abstract issues like democracy and tyranny are involved.

Conservation International uses dreamlike images of the ocean juxtaposed to rubbish washed up on the beach. The contrast is jarring and compels the audience to understand why the oceans are so important, be ready to take action to improve policy, change business practices, and make better choices in their daily lives.

The gesture and ink are similar but have entirely different emotional meanings.

Iraqi women feeling joyful, free, and defiant.

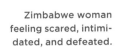

Zimbabwe woman feeling scared, intimidated, and defeated.

Case Study: Pastor John Ortberg
Emotive Storytelling

Storytelling creates the emotional glue that connects an audience to your idea. Creating unique, inspirational messages every week is demanding, and Pastor John Ortberg of Menlo Park Presbyterian relies heavily on his own life stories to illustrate his messages.

Ortberg's ability to weave stories into his messages is a big part of his trademark style and appeal. He spends as much time as he needs to word-craft and story-craft his messages together like a tapestry. He develops a master theme supported by Scripture, then carefully weaves personal stories throughout. It's very similar to the woof and warp of a loom. The master theme and Scripture hold the latitudinal messages together, and the stories are like the yarn that shuttles back and forth, creating patterns in the fabric.

The sermon analyzed on the next few pages was the first I heard Ortberg deliver. www I was intrigued by its structure and its ability to move me. The master theme was "people can bring the Kingdom of Heaven to this Earth by showing love." He sprinkled several stories through the sermon, but there was one master story that was referenced and carefully woven throughout: that of his sister's rag doll, Pandy. After telling the rag doll story (below) at the beginning, he continued to use it like glue with references to raggedness through-out the sermon.

The master story conveyed that people want to be loved in spite of their ragged condition:

"Now Pandy had lost most of her hair, one of her eyes, and one of her arms. But she was still my sister Barbie's favorite doll. She was not a very valuable doll. I don't think we could have given her away. She was not a very attractive doll. In fact, she was kind of a mess. But in the way that little kids do, for reasons that no one could quite understand, Barbie loved that little rag doll. So when Barbie ate, Pandy was next to her; when Barbie slept, Pandy was next to her; when Barbie took a bath, Pandy was next to her. Love Barbie, love her rag doll—it's a package deal. Other dolls came and went. Pandy was family.

"This is how strong that love went. One time, we took a vacation from Rockford, Illinois, up to Canada; and, of course, Pandy went with us. When we came back home, we realized Pandy had not made the return trip. Pandy had stayed in the hotel back in Canada. No other option was thinkable. My father turned the car around, and we drove from Rockford to Canada to get that doll because we were a devoted family. Not a very bright family, really, but a devoted family. And we tracked Pandy down.

"Pandy had never been worth very much to start with. By now, she was so disfigured that the only logical thing to do was to trash her. Get rid of her. But Barbie loved that doll with a love that made that doll precious to anybody that loved Barbie. Love Barbie, love her rag doll. It's a package deal.

"She did not love Pandy because Pandy was beautiful. She loved her with a love that *made* Pandy beautiful."

Ortberg ended his sermon by coming back to the premise of the opening story. Returning the congregation to the opening narrative took them to where they started with new, enlightened insights that made the story more meaningful and complete.

John Ortberg
Pastor, Menlo Park Presbyterian Church

Ortberg's Sparkline

Establish *What Could Be*
After telling the rag doll story, he equates it with how human love works on Earth versus the way heavenly love works on Earth. "There is a kind of love that seeks value in what is loved. There is a kind of love that is drawn to its object or a person because that person is attractive or that object is expensive or is important or can give me status or make me feel good. There is a kind of love that seeks value in what is loved, and there is a kind of love that creates value in what is loved."

Repeat the Theme
Ortberg jars the congregation a second time with the rag doll theme, saying that if you love God, you have to love His rag dolls, because nobody is perfect. "Jesus just kind of has one request. Christian faith is not real complex. We make it so complicated. It ain't rocket science. John puts it like this: '...[S]ince God so loved us, we ought also to love one another.' Jesus says, 'Love me, love my rag dolls.' It's a package deal. You can't have one without the other."

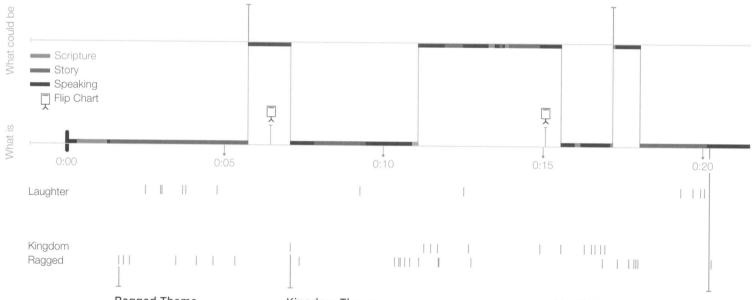

Ragged Theme
Ortberg uses phrases that emphasize concepts from the rag doll story to make the point that people are broken but still lovely and lovable.

Kingdom Theme
Ortberg uses the Kingdom as a master theme. Several times he contrasts the difference of how people love on Earth as opposed to the type of love expressed in the Kingdom of God.

Big Idea
Ortberg weaves story and Scripture together to convey his message but is careful to continually repeat his idea throughout his sermon. He brings the congregation back to the theme of love: "Wanna know how to break God's heart? Just don't love someone."

Call to Action

Ortberg concludes by convincing congregants that someone's value is determined by how loved they are. So he challenges them to call someone they hadn't yet told "I love you." "There is a kind of love that looks for value in what is loved, that looks for what is shiny and rich and impressive; but there is a kind of love that takes rag dolls and makes up there come down here ... Maybe you are aware right now there is somebody in your life that needs to hear you say, 'I love you.' Before the day is done, you need to look someone in the eyes, or you need to pick up the phone or pick up a pen. There are some words you need to say."

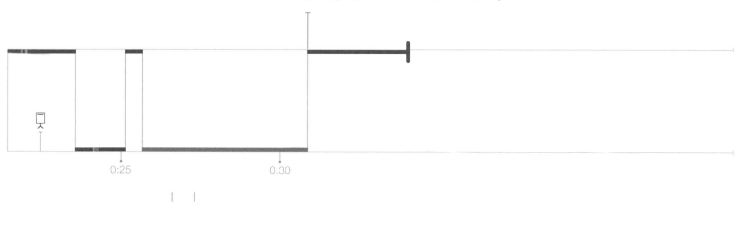

0:25   0.30

Emotional Moments

Ortberg chokes up twice during his sermon. Once when he repeats verses from an old song and again at the end of the sermon as he conveys the magnitude of what he's asking the congregation to do.

Case Study: Rauch Foundation
Shocking Statistics

In 2002, a small group of Long Island's civic, academic, labor, and business leaders gathered to discuss challenges facing the region and its potential for new directions. As a result of those meetings, The Rauch Foundation funded the Long Island Index to gather and publish data on the Long Island region. Their operating principle was "Good information presented in a neutral manner can move policy." The goal was to be a catalyst for action by engaging the community in thinking about its future from a regional perspective.

Even though the Long Island Index had served up valuable data about the past and present, the hope to drive action to make the future better hadn't seen much traction.

The local Long Island newspaper, *Newsday,* reported, "Last year, Index founder Nancy Rauch Douzinas challenged people to adopt a let's-do-something-about-this attitude. But the attitude, like action, hasn't materialized. So the Index is adopting an attitude of its own. It still will present data neutrally, and it won't take sides, but it will be much more active in trying to make sure that its ideas and its sense of urgency don't end when the lights come on after the annual presentation."[5]

So at the 2010 press launch of the Index, The Rauch Foundation pulled out key statistics and incorporated that information into a presentation. Dramatizing the key statistics with images helped convey the inventiveness and sense of urgency that would be required to manage growth with better environmental outcomes. Titled *The Clock is Ticking,* this four-and-a-half minute presentation showed one image after another to drive home the idea that Long Island is in steady decline and must do something—right now! www

"For seven years, the Long Island Index produced many reports filled with facts and figures that told people how poorly our region was faring. When we shifted to telling the story visually, the reaction was electric. The information was the same, but the new format communicated the issues with an emotional urgency. The visual story moved citizens and elected officials to address the problems with an understanding that there was no more time to lose."

Nancy Douzinas
President, Rauch Foundation

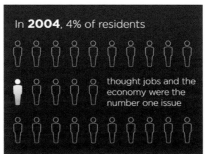

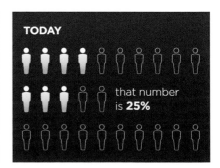

21% of Households...

Spend >50% **INCOME** on Housing

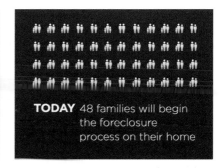

TODAY 48 families will begin the foreclosure process on their home

(WE ARE LOSING)

Our next generation of workers

22% of those aged 25–34 left Long Island between 2000 and 2008

69% of 18–34 year olds are somewhat or very likely to move within the next five years

Every **MINUTE**

$7,610

Every **MINUTE**

$7,610

is drained from our economy

THE CLOCK IS TICKING ON LONG ISLAND

Steve Jobs
CEO, Apple Inc.

Case Study: Steve Jobs
MacWorld 2007 iPhone Launch

Steve Jobs has the uncanny ability to make audience engagement appear simple and natural. His presentations compel an audience's undivided attention for an hour and a half or more—something that very few presenters can do.

"Steve Jobs does not deliver a presentation. He offers an experience."

Carmine Gallo[6]

Jobs's reputation for marketing brilliance already has the audience coming in to the presentation in a frenzied state of excitement, and he brilliantly keeps them there with dramatic suspense and an intriguing delivery. This is an uncommon skill for a CEO, or anyone, for that matter.

Jobs purposefully builds anticipation into each of his presentations—which have been described as an "incredibly complex and sophisticated blend of sales pitch, product demonstration, and corporate cheerleading, with a dash of religious revival thrown in for good measure."[7] **Over the years, he has used every type of S.T.A.R. moment. Below are four from his 2007 iPhone launch presentation.** www

- **Repeatable Sound Bites:** During the keynote address, Jobs used the phrase "reinvent the phone" five times, the same phrase that Apple used in their press release. After walking through the phone's features, he hammered it home once again: "I think when you have a chance to get your hands on it, you'll agree; we have reinvented the phone." The next day, *PC World* ran a headline stating that Apple would "reinvent the phone."[8]

- **Shocking Statistics:** Jobs didn't just state a large number; he put the scale of that number into a context the audience would understand. "We are selling over five million songs a day now. Isn't that unbelievable? Five million songs a day! That's fifty-eight songs every second of every minute of every hour of every day."

- **Evocative Visuals:** The audience laughed when he said, "Today Apple is going to reinvent the phone, and here it is...." He then showed an iPod faked-up to look like it had an old rotary dial on it to tease the audience.

- **Memorable Dramatization:** In the past, Jobs had pulled an iPod out of his coin pocket and removed a MacBook Air from an interoffice envelope. For this launch, a feature of the product itself created the dramatic moment. The new interface was so revolutionary that the audience gasped the first time he used the scrolling feature. Later, Jobs said, "I was giving a demo to somebody a little while ago at Apple. I finished the demo and I said, 'What do you think?' He told me this: 'You had me at scrolling.'"

Notice on page 164 to 165 how the bulk of his presentation centers on *what could be*. Not many presenters can sustain the momentum there, yet he keeps interest with a tightly rehearsed demo that showcases the revolutionary new features and demonstrates them in humorous and unexpected ways. See page 139 for a master list of ways to deliver contrast. Jobs incorporates many of these in his presentations too.

Note: Duarte Design does not work with Steve Jobs. This example was chosen for its historical significance as one of the greatest product launch presentations of all time.

Jobs's Sparkline

Establish *What Could Be*

"This is a day I've been looking forward to for two and a half years. Every once in a while, a revolutionary product comes along that changes everything. ... Today we're introducing three revolutionary products of this class. The first one is a widescreen iPod with touch controls. The second is a revolutionary mobile phone, and the third is the breakthrough Internet communications device. So three things: A widescreen iPod with touch controls, a revolutionary mobile phone, and a breakthrough Internet communications device. An iPod, a phone, and an Internet communicator. An iPod, a phone...are you getting it? These are not three separate devices. This is one device. And we are calling it iPhone."

Lure with Suspense

Jobs has a magical sense for creating suspense. For fifteen minutes, he reviews the hardware features of the iPhone by clicking through photos of the device while it is turned off. Yes, off! When he finally powers up the iPhone and demonstrates the scrolling feature for the first time, the audience gasps and breaks into roaring applause.

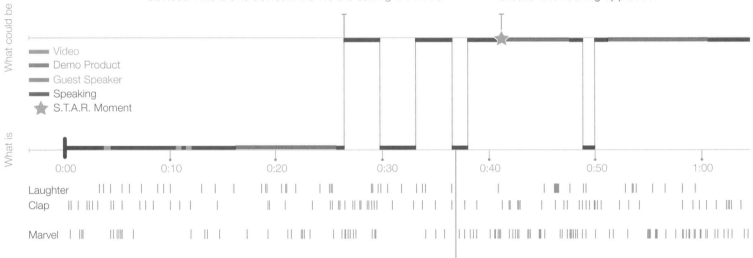

Establish *What Is*

Jobs sets up *what is* in perfect form. He gives an update on the market and performance of several products: Intel transition, retail stores, iPod, iTunes, and Apple TV. He demos the recently released Apple TV.

Create Contrast

Jobs comes back down to *what is* a few times in the speech by comparing the iPhone features with current products on the market that amplify the magnitude of this breakthrough.

Keep Them Engaged

When Jobs demos the new features, he doesn't merely go through a checklist of the features—he plans clever scenarios. Every thirty seconds or so, he showed a new feature by completing a task the way a real user would. He makes phone calls to a colleague while another colleague calls him; he checks his visual voicemail and plays a message from Al Gore congratulating him on the launch; he calls Starbucks to order four thousand lattes to go. He varied the tasks in his demo forty-seven times to make it a riveting demonstration.

The New Bliss

Jobs ends his presentation having enthusiastically moved his audience from *what is* to *what could be*. But he doesn't stop there. He reminds them of Apple's revolutionary product heritage and assures them that they'll do this again. His ending sets the stage for a new beginning. "I didn't sleep a wink last night. I was so excited about today because we've been so lucky at Apple. We've had some real revolutionary products. The Mac in 1984 is an experience that those of us that were there will never forget, and I don't think the world will forget it either. The iPod in 2001 changed everything about music. We're going to do it again with the iPhone in 2007. We're very excited about this. There's an old Wayne Gretzky quote that I love: 'I skate to where the puck is going to be, not where it has been.' We've always tried to do that at Apple since the very, very beginning, and we always will. Thank you very, very much."

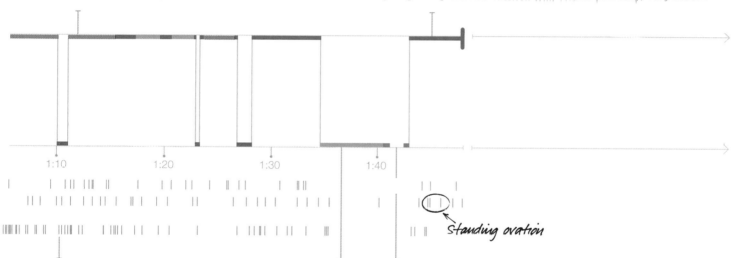

1:10   1:20   1:30   1:40

Standing ovation

Make Them Marvel

Jobs creates a sense of wonder by interjecting phrases that invite the audience to marvel at the product. A few examples of the language he uses: "This is a revolution of the first order—to really bring the real Internet to your phone! ... Isn't that great? ... So we think this is pretty cool. ...We've designed something wonderful for your hand, just wonderful. ... It's pretty awesome."

Invite Guest Speakers

Jobs invited three partners to present. The first two breezed through their parts but the Cingular/AT&T CEO read through cue cards, repeated what was already said, and rambled way longer than he should have. Too bad.

Be Flexible

When the clicker stops working, he pauses, smiles, and fills the time it takes to fix it with a funny story about how he and Steve Wozniak used a TV jammer as a prank on unsuspecting college students when they were in high school. Carmine Gallo said, "In this one-minute story, Jobs revealed a side of his personality that few people get to see. It made him more human, engaging, and natural. He also never got flustered."[9]

It's a great feeling to deliver a presentation after which everyone is buzzing with excitement at the watercooler; or your presentation is splashed on front-page news; or social media sites pick it up—and suddenly millions have seen your presentation.

The presentations that get repeated have memorable moments in them. These moments don't happen on their own; they are rehearsed and planned to have just the right amount of analytical and emotional appeal to engage both the minds and hearts of an audience.

Captivate your audience by planning a moment in your presentation that gives them something they'll always remember.

Memorable moments are
repeated and retransmitted
so they cover longer distances.

CHAPTER 8

There's Always Room to Improve

Amplify the Signal, Minimize the Noise

A presentation broadcasts information to an audience in much the same way that a radio broadcasts programming to listeners. Thus, the signal's strength and clarity determine how well information is conveyed to its intended recipients. Communication is a complex process that has many points at which the signal can break down. Once a message has left its sender, it is susceptible to interference and noise, which can cloud its intention and compromise the recipient's ability to discern the meaning.

Communication has the following parts: sender, transmission, reception, receiver, and noise. The message can become distorted at any step of this process. Your top priority is to ensure that the message-carrying signal is free from as much noise or interference as possible.

Presentation development works the same way. Every step of the process either enhances the signal or creates noise that causes the audience to tune out.

My own high-tech career began in 1984 selling custom high-frequency cable assemblies. Each cable was custom engineered to meet an extensive list of specifications. The task of every engineer and plant employee was to ensure that each step in the manufacturing process reduced the noise margin and protected the signal's quality. We tested raw materials, insulated wire with advanced materials, and produced gold-plated terminators. We fussed over everything at each stage and then tested everything before it was shipped. If it didn't fall within a tight impedance tolerance, we couldn't ship it, because it wouldn't work for the client's application. One small error would render the cable useless.

The same is true for creating a great presentation. The signal-to-noise ratio is an important factor in how well your message is received, and it's your job to minimize the noise. If the audience receives a message that includes any interference, they receive distorted information. You must expend energy minimizing the noise in each step of the communication process to ensure that a crystal-clear message gets through to your audience.

There are four main types of noise that can interfere with your signal: *credibility, semantic, experiential,* and *bias* noise. The graphic to the right shows where the various types of noise occur in communication. Your job is to minimize the noise as much as possible at each step of the process.

This section will address some of the factors that create noise. Noise can be reduced or eliminated through careful planning and rehearsing.

The Role of Noise in Communication[1]

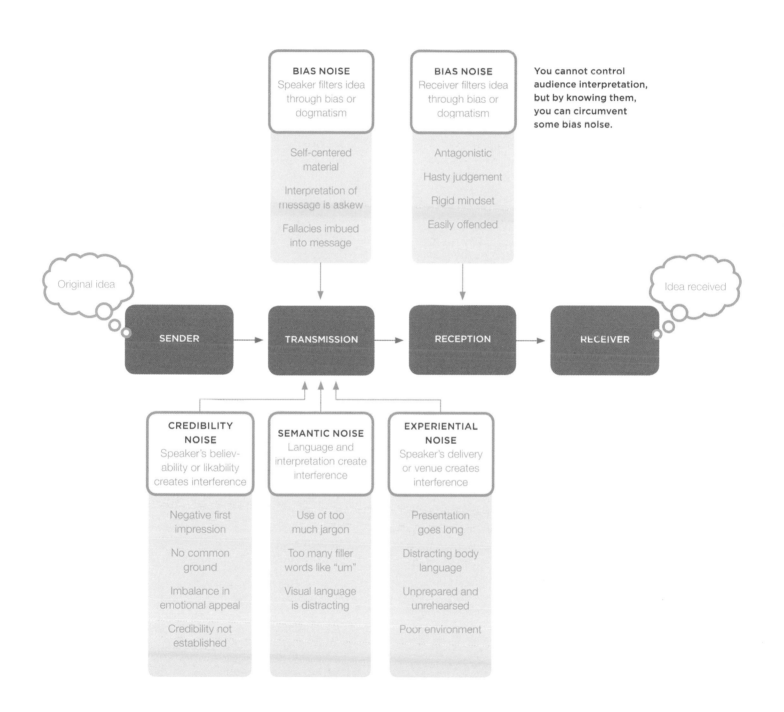

BIAS NOISE
Speaker filters idea through bias or dogmatism

Self-centered material

Interpretation of message is askew

Fallacies imbued into message

BIAS NOISE
Receiver filters idea through bias or dogmatism

Antagonistic

Hasty judgement

Rigid mindset

Easily offended

You cannot control **audience interpretation, but by knowing them, you can circumvent some bias noise.**

Original idea

SENDER

TRANSMISSION

RECEPTION

RECEIVER

Idea received

CREDIBILITY NOISE
Speaker's believability or likability creates interference

Negative first impression

No common ground

Imbalance in emotional appeal

Credibility not established

SEMANTIC NOISE
Language and interpretation create interference

Use of too much jargon

Too many filler words like "um"

Visual language is distracting

EXPERIENTIAL NOISE
Speaker's delivery or venue creates interference

Presentation goes long

Distracting body language

Unprepared and unrehearsed

Poor environment

Give a Positive First Impression

The old adage is true: You never get a second chance to make a first impression. But is telling a joke or using a cheesy icebreaker really the way to start?

Make some creative choices before the presentation begins. What is the first thing you want your audience to experience? What's the first impression you want them to have? In what kind of mood should your introduction put them? These choices aren't driven only by what you say. Moods can be set by the type of room, lighting, music playing, items on the chairs, image projected on the screen, clothing you're wearing, or entrance you make.

No matter how much you want the audience to like you for your mind and not for how you look, their first impression—for a while, at least—is based on what they see. **Within the first few seconds, people will classify you somewhere in their minds and judge whether they will be able to connect with you or not.**

Aristotle argued against letting first impressions influence the perceived validity of the content. He said, "Trust… should be created by the speech itself, and not left to depend upon an antecedent impression that the speaker is this or that kind of man." In ancient Greece, however, oration was very sophisticated and followed many rules. Most people in today's audiences are a bit more shallow and will use the first few crucial seconds to judge you.

Fear of being judged makes so many people afraid of public speaking. But it's in your power to shape that first impression. Don't allow yourself to be intimidated. You'd be amazed to hear what's on the audience's minds before you begin your presentation. With the advent of social media, you can see—and take comfort in—just how shallow and mindless the stream is. These are actual comments made by an audience while waiting for a presentation to begin: "Scalding hot coffee in a room packed with socially inept people means I now have a burned hand." "I hope there's no line in the ladies room." "I hope she has gone to Toastmasters since the last time she spoke." "Aw, man, I missed mimosas at registration this morning."

Yep, that's the stuff on their minds before you present. Their expectations are pretty low and self-focused, so creating a memorable first impression with these folks shouldn't be too tough.

First impressions do not have to be overly dramatic or gimmicky. They're about revealing your character, motivations, abilities, and vulnerabilities. You're asking the audience to walk in your shoes, and they don't even know if they like you yet, let alone your taste in shoes. So establishing who you are and your own likability is paramount.

Be aware that part of the first impression the audience has formed about you had already been made before you entered the room. Consider all the communications you sent before the presentation. What was the invitation like? How was the agenda framed? How was the e-mail worded? What was your bio like? Since all the interactions leading up to the actual presentation create the real first impression, make sure you've framed them appropriately.

Successful first impressions introduce you and your message in a way with which the audience can identify. It's the nature of all audiences to compare themselves to you and look for similarities and differences. Make these similarities and differences clear as they size you up, so they get over that phase quickly. Create a common identity between you and them.

This is my "do you really think I have time for this" look.

The audience learns a lot about you based solely on how you appear for the first time.

When I first started hosting *Slide:ology* workshops here at Duarte Design, I kept trying to squeeze an entire workday in before the workshop started at 9:00 AM. I'd blast into the room, test the projector, cross-check files, and jump into the material. I was busy, distracted, and wound up pretty tight. Any of the poor early birds got a clear "I'm super busy and was trying to squeeze in an entire workday before you got here" message. I noticed that the crowd wasn't warm or receptive to me.

Then, I attended a workshop hosted by a friend of mine and author of *Presentation Zen*, Garr Reynolds. Before his presentation, he entered the room upbeat and engaged, shook hands, asked attendees questions, and set a completely different tone. They perceived that he had all the time in the world for them. Right off the bat, he came across as carefree and warm. Even though our content was of similar nature, he had them eating out of his hands before he said the first word, and I didn't.

This is my "I have all the time in the world for you" look.

Hop Down from Your Tower

Have you ever sat through a presentation where—even though the presenter sounded super smart—you had no idea what he was really saying?

Most highly specialized fields like those in science and engineering have a distinct lexicon that's used every day—one that's familiar to experts but foreign to anyone not in that field. **Innovation is happening very quickly, and each new field generates a plethora of new terms weekly. If you're an expert, you can't assume that people have kept up with your field.** Using highly specialized jargon when you're addressing nonspecialists can hamper your efforts and reduce the amount of help you receive from them—solely because they don't understand what you're saying. You need to modify your language so it resonates with the potential collaborators and funders of your idea.

Before specialists acquired their newfangled vocabulary, they used the common language of the masses. But as they studied their narrow fields, specialized terms and jargon snuck in. It's like the folks who built the Tower of Babel. Originally, they all spoke a unified language. But due to their pride, their language was confused and they were scattered throughout the earth.

When presenting to a broad audience, you need to go back to a common and unified language so your audience doesn't scatter in confusion. Even though it's fun to sound smart—and yes, to confound others with your awesome smarty-pantness—this hinders the adoption of your idea when you're speaking to a group that isn't as specialized as you.

"Speaking in jargon carries penalties in a society that values speech free from esoteric, incomprehensible bullshit. Speaking over people's heads may cost you a job or prevent you from advancing as far as your capabilities might take you otherwise."

Carmine Gallo[2]

If your idea requires the use of special terminology, you must be prepared to translate it into intelligible words that laymen can understand. It's imperative that you know how and when to switch between specialized and common language. Don't choose words that fall outside your listener's vocabulary.[3] Tailor your language to what the audience uses.

For example, a great Nobel Laureate in Physiology, Barbara McClintock, discovered in the 1940s that genes are responsible for turning physical characteristics on or off. However, her groundbreaking research was greeted with skepticism and wasn't fully understood until the 1970s because of her communication style. McClintock had a vivid inner vision and a rapid-fire delivery. She would often leap back and forth from microscopic observation to model to conclusion to result—all in a single sentence! Most audiences were ill-prepared, or simply too lazy, to work hard enough to master the data that poured forth from her. The way she communicated caused her findings to lie hidden for years![4]

Jargon isn't confined to specialized professions. Many good ideas die because they fail to navigate the very organization from which they originate. Different departments within the same entity often use different languages, which can create internal confusion. In some meetings, more acronyms are spoken than real words.

An audience will not adopt your idea unless they understand it. **Your idea's perceived value will be judged not so much on the idea itself but on how well you can communicate it.**

Value Brevity

Presentations fail because of too *much* information, not too little. Don't parade in front of the audience spewing every factoid you know on your topic. Only share the right information for that exact moment with that specific audience.

Abraham Lincoln constructed the Gettysburg Address with 278 words and delivered it in just over two minutes. Though one of the shortest speeches in history, it is also considered to be one of the greatest.

The speech's purpose was to dedicate the Gettysburg cemetery and eulogize the fallen. Though eulogists at that time traditionally took hours, Lincoln was so quick that the photographers were still setting up their equipment as he finished; hence we have no photos of him delivering the speech.

Most people aren't even aware that Lincoln wasn't the featured speaker that day. Edward Everett shared the platform and delivered a eulogy in the traditional style, spending two hours praising the virtues of the soldiers. The day after the speech, Lincoln received a note from Everett that complimented him for the "eloquent simplicity and appropriateness" of his remarks. Everett said, "I should be glad, if I could flatter myself that I came as near to the central idea of the occasion, in two hours, as you did in two minutes."[5]

Lincoln had two hours and took two minutes. This forced him to make the central ideas clear. Even though it's brief, Lincoln's address still covers the key components of the presentation form. He discusses *what is* by stating historical national values, the current war situation, and the purpose of the gathering. He startles the audience by claiming that they cannot dedicate or consecrate the ground, although that's what they thought they were there to do. Instead, he proposes a call to action: That the crowd resolve that the dead shall not have died in vain. He then describes the new bliss of a free nation.

One thing that will help you remain brief is to put your own constraint on the amount of time you present. Imposing a shorter time frame requires you to be succinct. If they give you an hour, target a talk at forty minutes. Restriction of time forces clear structure and a filtering-down process that leaves only imperative messages.

"If I am to speak for ten minutes, I need a week for preparation; if fifteen minutes, three days; if half an hour, two days; if an hour, I am ready now."

Woodrow Wilson

3

NEW BLISS

It is rather for us to be here dedicated to the great task remaining before us—that from these honored dead we take increased devotion to that cause for which they gave the last full measure of devotion—that we here highly resolve that these dead shall not have died in vain —that this nation, under God, shall have a new birth of freedom—and that government of the people, by the people, for the people, shall not perish from the earth.

Call to Action

1

WHAT IS

Four score and seven years ago our fathers brought forth on this continent, a new nation, conceived in Liberty, and dedicated to the proposition that all men are created equal.

Now we are engaged in a great civil war, testing whether that nation, or any nation so conceived and so dedicated, can long endure. We are met on a great battlefield of that war. We have come to dedicate a portion of that field, as a final resting place for those who here gave their lives that that nation might live. It is altogether fitting and proper that we should do this.

2

WHAT COULD BE

But, in a larger sense, we can not dedicate—we can not consecrate—we can not hallow—this ground. The brave men, living and dead, who struggled here, have consecrated it, far above our poor power to add or detract. The world will little note, nor long remember what we say here, but it can never forget what they did here. It is for us the living, rather, to be dedicated here to the unfinished work which they who fought here have thus far so nobly advanced.

Wean Yourself from the Slides

Any slides you use during your presentation should serve as a stage setting or backdrop; they should rarely be the sole focus for the message. You, not the slides, deliver the message. **People can only process one inbound message at a time. They will either listen to you or read your slides; they cannot do both.**[6]

When you open a slide application to create a new slide, the default format you're offered is appropriate for a report. If you fill the default master template with words, it will take your audience twenty-five seconds to read the slide. Since they can't read and listen at the same time, if you have forty slides multiplied by twenty-five seconds, they'll be reading for over sixteen minutes of your presentation instead of listening to you.

By planning the structure first, you can ensure the presentation won't go too long. Audiences squirm when a frustrated presenter delivers for fifty-five minutes and then says, "Oh, man, where'd the time go? I still have forty-three slides, so hang on. I'll get through them in the next five minutes." If you plan a solid structure with the time frame in mind, it guarantees you will stay within the time constraints.

What's the right number of slides? There is no definitive "right" number of slides for a presentation. It's all driven by the personal delivery and pacing of the presenter. So the answer is "as many as necessary to get your point across." Hollywood scene and story analysts adhere to the practice of making scenes no longer than three minutes for fear of losing the audience's interest.[7]

Three minutes! Odds are high that your audience is losing interest every three minutes too, and to compound the problem, you don't have a $100 million blockbuster movie budget. Because the presentation medium is more static than cinema, don't stay on a slide for any more than two minutes. Changing the visuals as often as possible helps retain audience attention.

Most presentations have multiple points per slide and are a document, not a slide. If you choose to put only one idea per slide, you'll have more slides than are traditionally seen in a slide deck and that's okay.

I was invited to speak for forty-five minutes at a luncheon keynote. The organizers asked for the slides to be submitted thirty days in advance, so I crafted the message, rehearsed it, and sent a deck with 128 slides.

A week before my talk, I got a call from the organizers telling me that the keynote was reduced to twenty minutes and to resubmit slides. So I trimmed, rehearsed, and timed it for twenty minutes. The day of the presentation, the emcee reminded me to "stay within the forty-five minute slot because people enjoy a Q&A." Shocked, I told him that they'd reduced the speaking slot to twenty minutes. "No, you have an hour. We just told you twenty minutes because you had too many slides and we thought you'd go long." Internally, I was shouting, "I CREATE PRESENTATIONS FOR A LIVING," but on the outside, I smiled and said, "Well, there'll be a forty-minute Q&A. I hope they have a lot of questions."

Slide Content Reduction

There is a range of slide-content density. The number of words and amount of time it takes the audience to process the information determine whether you've created a dense document or a true visual aide to project onto the screen.

Your goal is to move away from projecting a document and toward giving a presentation. Only put elements on your slides that help the audience recall your message. Reduce large phrases and bodies of copy to single words. Simplify the slides so the audience can process each one in under three seconds. Remove as much from the slides as possible and move material into the notes. You can actually put as much information in the notes as you'd like.

Then, set up the slideshow to project the notes on the computer in front of you (Set Up Show/Show Presenter View). You can use the machine facing you as your teleprompter with all your notes in it, but behind you are projected clear, comprehensible slides for the audience. That way you won't miss a beat!

After hearing the advice to remove as much as possible per slide, many react with, "But my boss wants each of her direct reports to send in a five-slide overview of our initiatives, and if I make sparse slides, she might not understand the progress we've made." The boss is not asking for a presentation. She's asking for a document. So cram as much as you need into that document to make it clear. There's a time to be sparse per slide when you're presenting and a time to be comprehensive per slide when submitting a document.

When slides are used appropriately, they work with the presenter seamlessly like a dance partner on the stage. One is coming and the other going, and each contributes to the other's stage presence and craft. Practice with your slides until you move as one with them.

TELEPROMPTER

Use your computer as a teleprompter by having it display your notes.

VISUAL AIDE

Only project material on the screen that helps the audience remember your message.

Balance Emotion

Persuasive presentations should appropriately balance analytical and emotional appeal.

Many pages in this book have been devoted to creating emotional appeal—not because it's more important but because it's underused or nonexistent and *should* be incorporated. Now that your presentation has plenty of emotional appeal, let's stay cognizant of its appropriate use.

Some topics are inherently emotionally charged—like gun control, racism, or abortion—and therefore naturally lend themselves to more emotional arguments. On the other hand, topics like science, engineering, finance, and academics inherently invite analytical appeals. But just because a presentation is more heavily weighted toward analytical content doesn't mean it should be void of all emotion.

A question that comes up often is "How much emotion should I use when presenting to a group of economists?" (You can replace the word *economist* with others like *analysts*, *scientists*, *engineers*, or *researchers*.) Some people choose their careers because of their analytical

nature. If you know the audience has a career in a stereotypically analytical space, only a tiny percentage of your appeal should be emotional—but do not leave emotion out entirely! At the very least, open and close your presentation with *why*. Many times the reason *why* people are involved in economics or science or engineering or research has an emotional component. Don't strip it out, but don't overdose on it either.

There's another Greek word in the mix, in addition to *ethos, pathos,* and *logos* (see page 100). That word is *karios.* It means "timing" or "timeliness"—"speaking in the right moment, in the right way." In order to do this, you must understand the situation, cross-check, and, if necessary, modify your presentation by adjusting its emotional and analytical balance so that it's appropriate.

Keep in mind that all things in life should be done in moderation—including emotional appeal. Emotion should not be overamplified. If it is, the audience will feel manipulated. Appealing to emotion is only effective if it furthers the argument. Creating the right balance is alluring, whereas imbalance hurts your credibility.

Modify the presentation to map to the needs of the audience. Increase or decrease the emotional and analytical to match the situation.[8]

	BROAD AUDIENCE	ANALYTICAL AUDIENCE
Mode of response	Visceral	Cerebral
Structure	Weighted toward story	Weighted toward report
Responds to emotion	Receptive	Suspicious
Effective organs	Heart, gut, groin	Head

Instead of viewing the rhetorical triangle as something that is static and must be evenly filled in to achieve perfect balance on all sides, consider it dynamic and alter the emotional appeal appropriately based on the situation. If you're speaking to a broad audience on an emotionally charged topic, then don't go through pages and pages of analytical research. Pull back on the brainy material. When speaking to a specialized audience in a narrowly analytical field, you need to emphasize analytical content. Notice in the far-right triangle how imbalance will diminish your credibility.

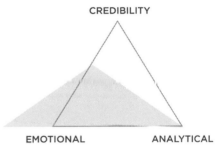

Highly analytical audiences do not like having their heartstrings tugged too much, if at all. They tend to interpret it as manipulation and an unnecessary waste of time. But these folks are human, and all humans care, like to laugh, and can be touched deeply. So, for example, including material in a presentation that shows how lives will be changed does motivate them, unless it's presented in a melodramatic way.

Emotionally driven audiences don't enjoy overuse of facts and details. They want to know that the details have been carefully considered, but they probably don't want to see twenty slides about them. They need a few proof points. A sales force might get more fired up about the incentive plan than diagrams explaining the complex innards of how a product ticks.

Taking the emotional or analytical appeal too far in either direction hurts your credibility. Even if you are the most qualified presenter in the world, being too geeky or too emotional can create a chasm between you and the audience.

Notice with the two triangles on the left, the credibility of the speaker stayed intact. That's because these presentations hit the right balance for the audience.

Host a Screening with Honest Critics

We've become a first-draft culture. Write an e-mail. Send. Write a blog entry. Post. Write a presentation. Present. The art of crafting and then recrafting something well is disappearing in communications.

"The first draft of anything is shit."

Ernest Hemingway

It's easy for us to get attached to our own ideas, so it's good to have another set of eyes and ears to review them. The best way to get feedback is to host a screening to test your messages before you present. The screening should filter out any meandering structure, obstructed messages, and confusing language.

Keep an open mind and come to the screening knowing that you will probably need to rework some percentage of the communication that you labored over for so long. No one ever hears during the first review, "I wouldn't change a thing." Regardless of how relentlessly you worked, there will be changes at this phase. The information was created from your perspective. To the degree you are receptive to feedback *from* others, you'll be able to refine the receptivity potential of your material *for* others. The screening should influence and round out how you deliver your presentation.

Conway's Law states, "Any organization that designs a system will inevitably produce a design whose structure is a copy of the organization's communication structure." In other words, the quality of communication your organization generates is limited to the quality of the communication of the organization itself. For this reason, **a presentation's quality will not exceed the quality of the planning process that precedes it.** Therefore, pulling together a team who will give you honest, helpful

feedback for the screening may require you to go outside of your organization.

Remove yourself from a sugar-sweet or dysfunctional review environment. Instead, pull together a small group that has a similar profile as your target audience. They could be people in your industry like analysts, internal employees, trusted customers, or a focus group. Choose naysayers who will scrutinize, criticize, and challenge your perspective. You want them to be brutally honest when they tell you what they think.

Each screener should have a printout of the slides and notes of your presentation so they can quickly jot down thoughts on the words and the visuals. Run through the entire presentation once and then revisit each section carefully. A solid review meeting should last about three times as long as the presentation itself. If your presentation is twenty minutes long, for example, each screening should take an hour. If your presentation lasts an hour, the screening should take three.

Find someone as far away from your twisted environment as possible to give honest feedback.

Give your test audience a safe environment to tell you what they *really* think. Solicit feedback in a nondefensive way and let them challenge all assumptions. Encourage them to tell you whether your presentation genuinely kept their interest.

Don't ignore your screeners' insights or give "yeah, but..." or "if they really knew..." excuses. *Really* listen to them and incorporate their insights. Then, rework your material. Screening the presentation will remove any burrs that would unintentionally snag or poke the audience with misunderstandings.

These negative organizational systems, illustrated below, limit the quality of your communication. If you work in any of these communication environments, go outside your organization to get honest, constructive feedback on your presentation.

CONCEITED CAPTAIN: Leader engages late and forces team into time-crunched, low-quality output.

POLITICAL PARANOIA: No one makes progressive decisions out of fear for their own destruction.

MESSAGE MAGIC: In the absence of a strategy, imaginary messages become the norm. (See page 199)

VACUUM VISIONARY: There's no room for alternative perspectives, and subject matter experts have no seat at the table.

LACKEY LEADER: Indecisive leadership and flattery-driven consensus stalls strategy traction.

CUSTOMER COLD-SHOULDER: Self-focused communication is valued more highly than customer insight.

Case Study: Markus Covert, PhD
Pioneer Award Winner

Thousands of the nation's top scientists apply for the Pioneer Award, sponsored by the National Institute of Health. The winners usually have high-risk, high-reward ideas that will transform how medical research is performed. Finalists travel to Maryland to deliver a fifteen-minute presentation followed by fifteen minutes of Q&A. Presentations are delivered to a panel of top-notch scientists who may or may not be in the same field of study, which means the ideas have to be conveyed in a way that resonates with a scientist in any field.

Markus Covert, PhD, assistant professor of bioengineering at Stanford University, was the 2009 winner of a grant for $2.5 million. He strongly believes that the amount of feedback and practice he put into his presentation is what sealed the deal for him.

Everything in Covert's presentation had to justify his hypothesis and warrant its funding. He needed to include the big picture but also dive deep in places to prove that he was knowledgeable. Covert challenged a long-standing scientific-communication tradition by incorporating emotional appeal in his presentation. He wanted the tone to be inspirational in addition to instructive—a brave departure from cerebral scientific traditions. Adding such a visceral layer was counterintuitive; he knew even a thin veneer of emotional appeal would go a long way. So instead of focusing solely on *how*, he included content about *why* his project would change scientific research.

Knowing his approach was risky, Covert rehearsed the presentation twenty different times with scientists in various disciplines. Twenty. Following his very scientific nature, he systematically presented over and over to scientists from various backgrounds, collected feedback, and modified the presentation to reflect their insights. At times, it was a struggle to add material while removing pieces of which he'd become fond, but Covert took a humble stance and was determined to embrace and implement the feedback.

It wasn't until he reached the nineteenth and twentieth rehearsal that the feedback was "Don't change a thing; it's perfect!" It was a lot of rehearsing, but he knew the material, and delivery had to be just right.

There is much about science that is inspiring. Often, the heartfelt passion gets buried in the facts and proofs. **By including emotion in his presentation and rehearsing it until it was just right, Covert won the grant.** He now gets to spend time in his lab pursuing his passion instead of worrying where the funding will come from.

Factoid: Covert is using his grant funds to pursue the Holy Grail of biology, which some have called the "ultimate test"—building a computer program that simulates an entire cell. If successful, his research could revolutionize our understanding and treatment of disease.

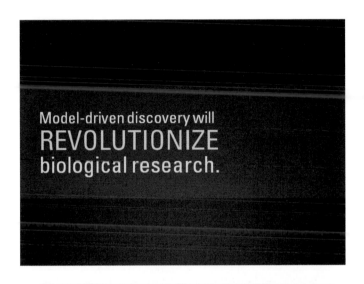

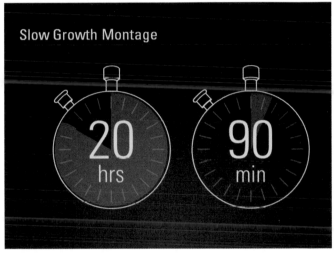

Covert used a clean minimalist design for his slides. Many scientific presentations clutter the slides with too much data. His were perfectly balanced.

"The original **energizing motor** that makes me compose is **the** urge to communicate—and to **communicate** with as many people as possible. Because **what** I love about the world and life is **people,** I like them as much as I like music, if **not more.** I love people, and I have a compul-**sion to share** with **people** what I feel, what I **know,** what I think."

Leonard Bernstein

Leonard Bernstein
Conductor, New York Philharmonic

Case Study: Leonard Bernstein
Young People's Concerts

Leonard Bernstein was a talented composer, conductor, pianist, teacher, and Emmy-winning television personality. He loved to talk about music and did so with everyone: friends, colleagues, teachers, students, and even children. Bernstein's unique intelligence and wit afforded him a reputation as music's most articulate spokesperson.[9] *Variety* magazine summed up his appeal by stating "The [New York] Philharmonic's conductor has the knack of a teacher and the feel of a poet. The marvel of Bernstein is that he knows how to grab attention and carry it along, measuring just the right amount of new information to precede every climax."[10]

Of all the things Bernstein accomplished, leading the Young People's Concerts was one of his proudest legacies. Several times a year, Carnegie Hall would fill with young children who came to learn about classical music. Bernstein would deliver a lecture-driven concert that could hold the attention of small children for an hour or more as he taught them complex music theory. **The lecture-concerts were successful because Bernstein put the same energy and discipline into them that he put into his music.** www

Bernstein's explanations, analogies, and metaphors were delivered in a clear, simple, yet poetic presentation that consistently stayed at the children's understanding level. He isolated various layers of the music, explained the theory behind it, played excerpts of it on the piano, and used various instrumentalists to play portions of it. Then, when the full piece was performed, the children had a clearer understanding of the many nuances.

Below are three excerpts from one of the most difficult musical subjects to explain, "What is Symphonic Music?" Bernstein uses items familiar to the children as metaphors:[11]

- "How does development actually work? It happens in three main stages, like a three-stage rocket going into space. The first stage is the simple birth of the idea, like a flower growing out of a seed. You all know the seed, for example, that Beethoven planted at the beginning of his [fifth] symphony, "dunt dunt dunt duuuunt." Out of it rises a flower that goes like this: <plays piano>"

- "[Brahms] puts two to three melodies together...and takes scraps of melodies and turns things upside down like pancakes. But it's not that it's upside down but that it sounds amazing upside down. Will it be beautiful? That's what makes Brahms so great. Music doesn't just change. It changes beautifully."

- "I'm hoping you'll hear it with new ears and hear the symphonic wonders of it, the growth of it, and the miracle of life in it that runs like blood through its veins and connects every note to every other note and makes it the great piece of music that it is."

Bernstein worked for days on his Young People's Concert scripts and rehearsed them several times so that when he was talking it would sound as if he were just having a calm, casual conversation with the children.

Bernstein put just as much rehearsal energy into his presentation scripts as he did into his musical scores.

Few of Bernstein's viewers were aware of how much dogged work went into his presentations. He was so adept at displaying an easy, casual manner that his presentations appeared to be born effortlessly and spontaneously. The truth, of course, was that he worked hard on his scripts. Weeks before, and right up to the last minute, his offices, house, and dressing rooms were filled with scattered piles of paper as he and his team wrote, planned, and rehearsed.[12]

Bernstein generated ideas on yellow legal pads and collaborated with his equally dedicated co-workers until a graceful, accessible script was formed.[13] The team would make sure each metaphor and allegory was appropriate for the audience. Bernstein himself would walk through the script several times, marking and rehearsing as he went.

Bernstein and his team edited constantly, right up to the moment he walked on stage. After each show, they would watch the recording of what he said and evaluate it to improve it the next time. He'd identify improvements he could make so he didn't commit the same mistakes over and over. While all good conductors review their concerts, Bernstein applied this practice to his presentations as well so that each one got better than the last.

Conductors are trained to have a disciplined rehearsal process, so editing a script through multiple iterations wouldn't be a foreign process for them. They read a musical score the way most people read a book. Paging through Bernstein's scores is like watching him rehearse. He studied and reviewed a score several times, working hard to represent the composer's intent. He had a special pencil that he used while reading scores that he called his "red-ee blue-ee" (one end wrote in red pencil, the other in blue). As he continued through the score, he flipped the pencil back and forth as he thought about the expression of the music from his point of view as the conductor or that of the individual musicians (his audience).[14]

The blue markings were conductor markings for Bernstein himself that helped identify phrasing, instrumental cues, and musical emphasis. The red markings were notes to the musicians that would be transferred to each of their specific parts. These markings are particularly interesting. He was a literary conductor that didn't just draw attention to a marking; he poetically described what he wanted the musician to feel. John Cerminaro, who played for years in the New York Philharmonic's horn section, said, "You couldn't just play a solo according to the notes on the page; [Bernstein] wanted something special on an emotional level every time."[15]

Bernstein tried to anticipate everything while he rehearsed and refined his presentation scripts. He planned every word and audience reaction carefully. He developed his scripts to the point of anticipating multiple audience responses—even writing alternate sections based on how people might react to the previous point. He even made notations of where and how he would stand while on the stage. The New York Philharmonic archives contain copies of scripts that show as many as ten revisions (in addition to the rounds on his yellow pads), which is a reflection of the thoroughness of Bernstein's thought process and rehearsals.[16]

Bernstein wrote about his Young People's Concerts experience in 1968 using words that can stand as his credo. "These concerts are not just concerts—not even in terms of the millions who view them [on TV] at home," he wrote. "They are, in some way, the quintessence of all I try to do as a conductor, as a performing musician. There is a lurking didactic streak in me that turns every program I make into a discourse, whether I utter a word or not; my performing impulse has always been to share my feelings, or knowledge, or speculations about music—to provide thought, suggest historical perspective, encourage the intersection of musical lines. And from this point of view, the Young People's Concerts are a dream come true, especially since the sharing is done with young people—that is, people who are eager, unprejudiced, curious, open, and enthusiastic."[17]

Regardless of your subject matter, passion and practice make perfect.

This excerpt from the script for "Humor in Music" shows how carefully Bernstein and his team planned.

```
22

                    BERNSTEIN  (CONT'D)
In music composers can make these
surprises in lots of different ways - by
making the music loud when you expect it
to be soft, or the other way around; or
by suddenly stopping in the middle of a
phrase; or by writing a wrong note on
purpose, a note you don't expect, that
doesn't belong to the music.  Let's try
one, just for fun.  You all know those
silly notes that go -
SING:  SHAVE AND A HAIRCUT - 2 BITS

O.K. Now you sing "Shave and a Haircut",
and the orchestra will answer you with
"2 bits" and see what happens.
ORCH:    ILLUSTRATE


(IF NO LAUGH)
Now, you see, you didn't laugh out loud.
(IF LAUGH)
Now most people don't laugh out loud about
musical jokes.  That's one of the things
about musical humor: you laugh inside.
Otherwise you could never listen to a
Haydn symphony: the laughter would drown
out the music.  But that doesn't mean a
Haydn symphony isn't funny.

ag               (MORE)
```

Practice makes perfect—kind of. An old adage says, "if anyone does not stumble in word, he is a perfect man." And no one is perfect. There is always room to improve. So be tenacious in preparing yourself ahead of time. Rehearse and re-rehearse. Then afterward, solicit feedback—and if it was taped, review the recording and then start the refinement process all over again.

Successful people plan and prepare. To be successful in any profession requires discipline and mastery of skills. Applying that same discipline to the skill of communication will attach the audience to your idea and improve your professional trajectory.

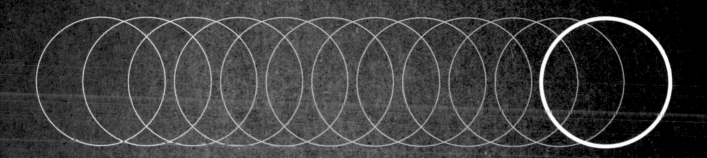

Audience interest is
directly proportionate to
the presenter's preparation.

CHAPTER 9

Change Your World

Changing the World Is Hard

If you say, "I have an idea for something," what you really mean is, "I want to change the world in some way." What is "the world" anyway? It is simply all of the ideas of all of our ancestors. Look around you. Your clothes, language, furniture, house, city, and nation all began as a vision in someone else's mind. Your food, drink, vehicles, books, schools, entertainment, tools, and appliances all came from someone's dissatisfaction with the world as they found it.[1] Humans love to create. And creating starts with an idea that can change the world.

Staying passionate and tenacious about your idea requires that some part of you be uncomfortable with the status quo. At times, you must have enough resolve to put your reputation on the line for the sake of advancing your idea. It's scary to go out on a limb and approach others with a product, philosophy, or ideal that you passionately support. Some will challenge it, and some will reject it. And that's hard. Society doesn't reward rejects, but it does reward those who have the tenacity to keep going after being rejected. So don't give up.

My husband and I collect large, oversized vintage posters. Once, while on vacation with our kids, we stopped in to see one of the poster dealers. He wore white cotton gloves as he carefully turned over each table-sized poster. When he turned to the poster on the right, both my kids gasped and said, "Oh my gosh, Mom. It's you! You have to buy that poster." Hmmm. Was it a good thing they felt that way?

The poster is an old French advertisement for baking spices. Baking spices! It's comical to see how fired up this gal is to promote her little collection of spices. But if I were to replace her pack of spices with the words "effective presentations," I guess this is me. I get pretty fired up.

Ideas are not really alive if they are confined to only one person's mind. Your idea becomes alive when it is adopted by another person, then another, and another, until it reaches a tipping point and eventually obtains a groundswell of support.

President Kennedy gave a speech declaring that by the end of the decade, the United States should land a man on the moon and bring him home safely. He wanted support from every American. He said in the speech, "In a very real sense, it will not be one man going to the moon—it will be an entire nation. For all of us must work to put him there." He wanted the entire country to feel responsible for supporting his vision. Later in the 1960s, JFK was touring NASA headquarters and stopped to talk to a man with a mop. The president asked him, "What do you do?" The janitor replied, "I'm putting the first man on the moon, sir." This janitor could have said, "I clean floors and empty trash." Instead, he saw his role as part of the bigger mission that was to fulfill the vision of the president. As far as he was concerned, he was making history.[2]

"The only reason to give a speech is to change the world."

John F. Kennedy

"There is one thing stronger than all the armies in the world, and that is an idea whose time has come."

Victor Hugo[3]

Use Presentations to Help Change the World

Presentations really can change the world. Who would have thought that a movie about a presentation would win an Academy Award, create global awareness, and incite change? Long before *An Inconvenient Truth* was on anyone's radar, former Vice President Al Gore had delivered his presentation hundreds of times to influential audiences around the world. In fact, he'd been delivering a similar presentation back as far as the 1970s.

You might not need to change the *entire* world, but you can definitely change your world using a presentation. Many of the people featured in this book delivered presentations over and over. They didn't just present once and call it a day. Their lives were spent constantly communicating their visions.

To see a systemic adoption of your idea, you may have to deliver multiple presentations. On your way to change the world, there will be key communication milestones that become catalysts for your success. Each milestone is an opportunity to adjust the strategy, collaborate, and realign the team. The brilliant discussions that occur when pulling a presentation together sometimes have as much value as the presentation itself.

Below are only a few of the milestones in a product launch that include a presentation. Each one represents a critical communication stage in the product's life cycle that is usually conveyed through a presentation.

Presentations play a valuable role throughout the life cycle of a product

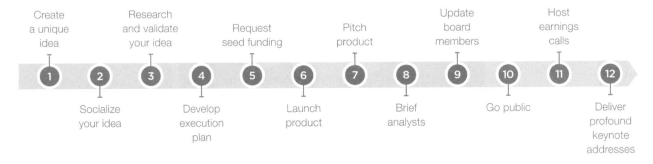

Create a unique idea	Research and validate your idea	Request seed funding	Pitch product	Update board members	Host earnings calls
1	3	5	7	9	11
2	4	6	8	10	12
Socialize your idea	Develop execution plan	Launch product	Brief analysts	Go public	Deliver profound keynote addresses

"If a business is really a decision factory, then the presentations that inform those decisions determine their quality."

Marty Neumeier[4]

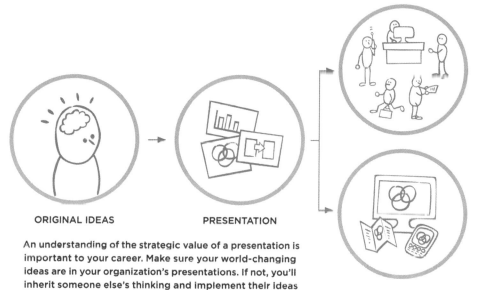

ACTIVITIES

After the ideas are presented and agreed to, work activities are generated from the presentations. Most presentations persuade people to take action, so presentations spawn a lot of activity.

MEDIA

Also, after the brilliant thinking in the presentation is solidified, it ripples through and informs other related materials needed to support and spread the idea like web sites, social media, brochures, and so forth.

ORIGINAL IDEAS   **PRESENTATION**

An understanding of the strategic value of a presentation is important to your career. Make sure your world-changing ideas are in your organization's presentations. If not, you'll inherit someone else's thinking and implement their ideas instead of influencing innovation with yours.

Remember, just because you communicated your idea once doesn't mean you're done. It takes several presentations delivered over and over to make an idea become reality. Well-prepared presentations will speed up the adoption and change your world!

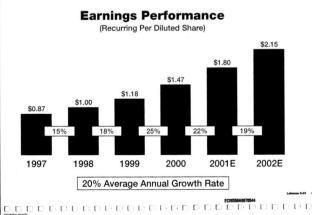

Earnings Performance
(Recurring Per Diluted Share)

$0.87 — 1997
$1.00 — 1998 (15%)
$1.18 — 1999 (18%)
$1.47 — 2000 (25%)
$1.80 — 2001E (22%)
$2.15 — 2002E (19%)

20% Average Annual Growth Rate

In mid-August 2001, Ken Lay presented this exact slide at an employee meeting to assure them that 2001 was fine and 2002 would be even better. Enron was valueless by the end of 2001. (Slide courtesy of the Department of Justice.)

Don't Use Presentations for Evil

Anyone who takes even a quick look at the hundreds of slides submitted as evidence in the Enron trial will see that presentations can play a conspicuous role in the perpetration of lies. Presentations are a powerfully persuasive tool that should be used for good and not evil.

Jeff Skilling (Chief Executive Officer), Kenneth Lay (Chairman of the Board), and Richard Causey (Chief Accounting Officer) all had several counts against them based on their presentations. All three were charged with ten counts each for their earnings-call presentations, and Ken Lay was charged with two counts for employee presentations. Because their presentations were transmitted into different states via phones and web technology, these executives were also charged with the federal crime of wire fraud. In fact, Skilling was sentenced to fifty-two months for *each* of the five counts involving presentations for which he was convicted.[5]

Presentations got these executives into this mess, while the *right* presentation could have prevented it altogether.

- **Scandal started with a presentation:** Andrew Fastow, Enron's chief financial officer, was the mastermind of clever accounting who used "special purpose entities" to hide billions of dollars and ultimately line his pockets with over $45 million. According to *USA Today,* Fastow gave "a slick presentation on the LJM partnerships" (the organization created to hide debt), and the "Enron managers and analysts stared at each other in confusion. It sounded too good to be true."[6] A slick presentation by a slick villain lured them into this mess.

- **Scandal could have been prevented with a presentation:** A detailed presentation given by Arthur Andersen's

David Duncan in February 1999 feebly warned the Enron Board of Director's audit committee of the company's risky accounting practices. This presentation could have saved Enron. If Duncan had boldly built a slide in capital letters saying "ENRON HAS RISKY PRACTICES THAT NEED INVESTIGATION," its demise might have been avoided. Instead, Duncan's notes found on the margin of his dense slide presentation said, "Obviously, we are on board with all of these [risks]."[7]

Enron's top executives played by their own rules. They made risky bets motivated by greed and ambition. The collapse was inevitable. As masters of the PowerPoint chart, they showed upward projections for sales and profits, encouraging employees to invest while they themselves were frantically removing their own money. Employees who raised questions were mysteriously moved to other departments. Skilling distracted investors by proposing bold strategies for the next big score, like entering the broadband and weather futures markets. (What's an oil company doing brokering weather, anyway?)

They aggressively designed communication that abandoned reason and truth altogether, and they used presentations as a propaganda device to spread lies to employees, analysts, and stockholders about Enron's performance. In the ensuing collapse, the credibility of the board and the executives involved was obliterated, and tens of thousands of employees were financially ruined.

Oral communications have built and toppled kingdoms. Presentations are a powerfully persuasive medium that should be used to build up—not tear down.

Enron's Presentations During Implosion

Out of the thousands of presentations given at Enron annually, many had direct implications in Enron's demise. This chart highlights several that played a role in the scandal.

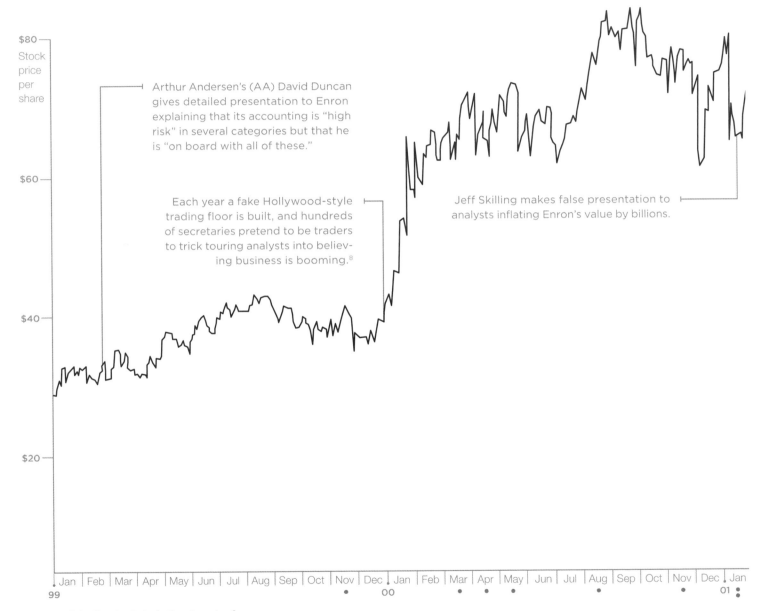

Arthur Andersen's (AA) David Duncan gives detailed presentation to Enron explaining that its accounting is "high risk" in several categories but that he is "on board with all of these."

Each year a fake Hollywood-style trading floor is built, and hundreds of secretaries pretend to be traders to trick touring analysts into believing business is booming.[8]

Jeff Skilling makes false presentation to analysts inflating Enron's value by billions.

• = Intentional acts to further the crime[9]

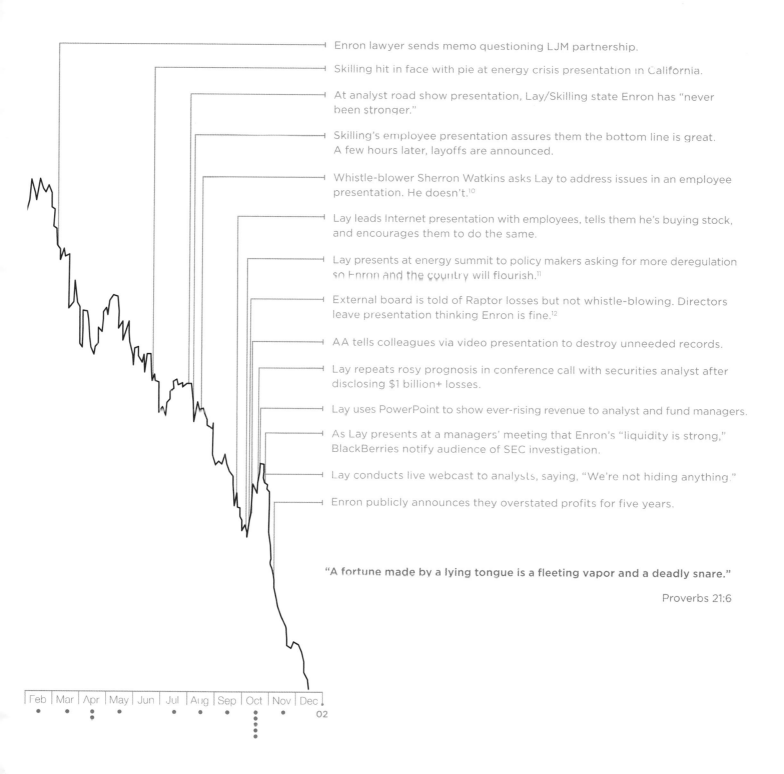

Enron lawyer sends memo questioning LJM partnership.

Skilling hit in face with pie at energy crisis presentation in California.

At analyst road show presentation, Lay/Skilling state Enron has "never been stronger."

Skilling's employee presentation assures them the bottom line is great. A few hours later, layoffs are announced.

Whistle-blower Sherron Watkins asks Lay to address issues in an employee presentation. He doesn't.[10]

Lay leads Internet presentation with employees, tells them he's buying stock, and encourages them to do the same.

Lay presents at energy summit to policy makers asking for more deregulation so Enron and the country will flourish.[11]

External board is told of Raptor losses but not whistle-blowing. Directors leave presentation thinking Enron is fine.[12]

AA tells colleagues via video presentation to destroy unneeded records.

Lay repeats rosy prognosis in conference call with securities analyst after disclosing $1 billion+ losses.

Lay uses PowerPoint to show ever-rising revenue to analyst and fund managers.

As Lay presents at a managers' meeting that Enron's "liquidity is strong," BlackBerries notify audience of SEC investigation.

Lay conducts live webcast to analysts, saying, "We're not hiding anything."

Enron publicly announces they overstated profits for five years.

"A fortune made by a lying tongue is a fleeting vapor and a deadly snare."

Proverbs 21:6

Feb | Mar | Apr | May | Jun | Jul | Aug | Sep | Oct | Nov | Dec

02

Gain Competitive Advantage

In life, someone's always winning, and someone's always losing. This isn't just true in commerce. Even beliefs and values go through seasons of victory and defeat. There's a constant push and pull related to what's perceived as right or wrong, based solely on how it's communicated.

Most communicators are visionaries who can see where to go and how to get there. An executive "sees" where the company needs to go; a manager "sees" how to build a strategy; an engineer "sees" how to construct a product; and a marketer "sees" how to promote it. Even our social causes are "seen" before they are solved. Your job as a communicator is to get others to "see" what you are saying so your ideas gain traction. If you can do that, you win.

I recently had dinner with a friend who works for a top international consulting firm. His group was competing for a multimillion-dollar piece of business against another leading firm. They pulled together their smartest team and delivered a brilliant presentation, and they were shocked to get the news that they didn't win the business. The reason? Even though the client confirmed that my friend's firm was smarter, the client couldn't understand the findings. Their brilliance was obscured by dense, smart-sounding slides. My friend's firm did smarter work; however, the other firm communicated its findings in a way that was useful. All the smarts in the world are useless if they are not understood.

Getting stakeholders to understand your ideas—while the competitor's concepts remain obscure—ensures a victory. **If presented well, a smart idea acts as the igniting spark for an explosion of human and material resources.** A great presentation gives smart ideas an advantage.

If your presentation is great, it can become a broadly reaching social media phenomenon. Now, more than any other time in history, great presentations transcend the moment in which they're given, because they can be seen by millions of people who weren't there in person. Your presentation can be viewed over and over again, long after you gave it. Randy Pausch's last lecture has been seen on YouTube over 12 million times. The website TED.com hosts eighteen-minute-long presentations and has had over 100 million views. Martin Luther King Jr.'s "I Have a Dream" speech has been watched over 15 million times on YouTube. Those numbers are big enough to start a movement. When a presentation is great and is recorded, people will watch it again and again.

If your message is clear and worth repeating, it will be repeated. If your message is repeated, you win! Sound simple? It is.

Case Study: Martin Luther King Jr.
His Dream Became Reality

Martin Luther King Jr. was one of the greatest orators and civil rights activists in U.S. history. His goal was to end racial segregation and discrimination using peaceful means.

King delivered his electrifying "I Have a Dream" speech from the steps of the Lincoln Memorial during the 1963 March on Washington, which became the flash point for a movement.

Insights from "I Have a Dream":

The sparkline on the next few spreads includes a full transcript of the speech to help identify the following insights:

- **Contour:** King's speech moves between *what is* and *what could be* rapidly, which is an appropriate pace for the heightened energy of the gathering.

- **Dramatic pauses:** The sparkline has a line break for each time he pauses. As you're reading it, breathe for a second or two at the end of each line to get a sense of how it was spoken.

- **Repetition:** King uses the rhetorical device of repetition often. Throughout the speech, he repeats word sequences to create emphasis. Toward the end, he repeats the phrase "I Have a Dream" several times, like the refrain of a hymn.

- **Metaphor/visual words:** King masterfully uses descriptive language to create images in the mind. For example, he states, "Now is the time to rise from the dark and desolate valley of segregation to the sunlit path of racial justice."

- **Familiar songs, Scripture, and literature:** King establishes common ground by referencing many spiritual hymns and Scriptures familiar to the audience. He even rephrases a small sequence from Shakespeare: "This sweltering summer of the Negro's legitimate discontent will not pass until there is an invigorating autumn…"

- **Political references:** King pulls lines from several political resources like the U.S. Declaration of Independence, the Emancipation Proclamation, the U.S. Constitution, and the Gettysburg Address.

- **Applause:** There are varying degrees of applause throughout ranging from clapping to clapping with loud cheering. In the sixteen-minute speech, the audience applauds twenty-seven times. That's applause approximately every thirty-five seconds.

- **Pacing:** King speeds up and slows down to vary the quantity of words spoken per minute. This creates three distinct bursts or crescendos in his speech that build to the passionate ending that describes the new bliss.

King's speech heightened the awareness of civil rights issues across the country, bringing more pressure on Congress to advance civil rights legislation and end racial segregation and discrimination.

In 1963, King was named *Time* magazine's Man of the Year. A short forty-six years later, the United States elected its first African American president, Barack Obama.

Great communicators create movements.

Listen along at www as King delivers his speech.

Martin Luther King Jr.
Civil Rights Activist

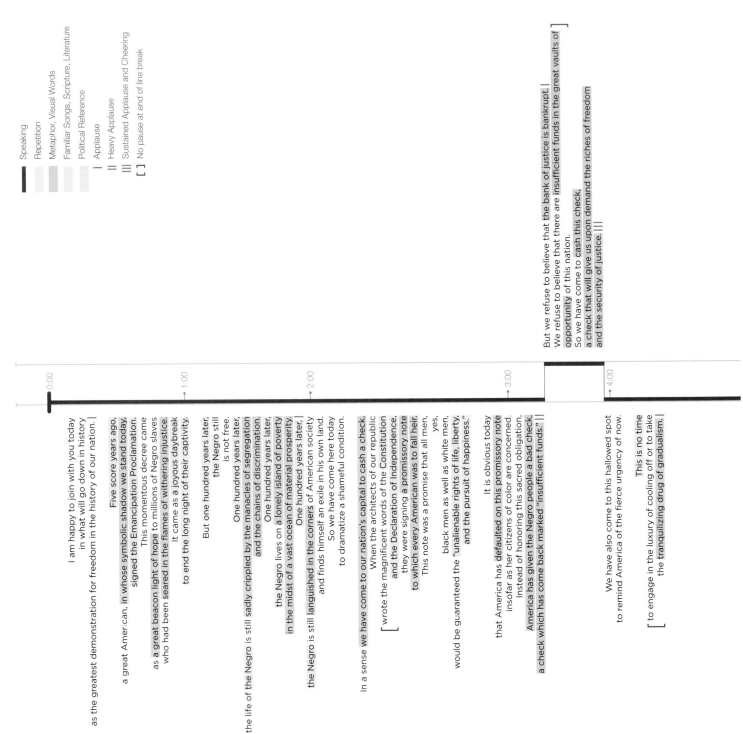

Speaking
Repetition
Metaphor, Visual Words
Familiar Songs, Scripture, Literature
Political Reference
| Applause
‖ Heavy Applause
‖‖ Sustained Applause and Cheering
[ ] No pause at end of line break

What could be

What is

0:00   1:00   2:00   3:00   4:00

I am happy to join with you today
in what will go down in history
as the greatest demonstration for freedom in the history of our nation. |

Five score years ago,
a great American, in whose symbolic shadow we stand today,
signed the Emancipation Proclamation.
This momentous decree came
as a great beacon light of hope to millions of Negro slaves
who had been seared in the flames of withering injustice.
It came as a joyous daybreak
to end the long night of their captivity.

But one hundred years later,
the Negro still
is not free.
One hundred years later,
the life of the Negro is still sadly crippled by the manacles of segregation
and the chains of discrimination.
One hundred years later,
the Negro lives on a lonely island of poverty
in the midst of a vast ocean of material prosperity.
One hundred years later, |
the Negro is still languished in the corners of American society
and finds himself an exile in his own land.
So we have come here today
to dramatize a shameful condition.

In a sense we have come to our nation's capital to cash a check.
When the architects of our republic
[wrote the magnificent words of the Constitution
and the Declaration of Independence,
they were signing a promissory note
to which every American was to fall heir.
This note was a promise that all men,
yes,
black men as well as white men,
would be guaranteed the "unalienable rights of life, liberty,
and the pursuit of happiness."

It is obvious today
that America has defaulted on this promissory note
insofar as her citizens of color are concerned.
Instead of honoring this sacred obligation,
America has given the Negro people a bad check,
a check which has come back marked "insufficient funds." ‖

But we refuse to believe that the bank of justice is bankrupt. |
We refuse to believe that there are insufficient funds in the great vaults of [
opportunity of this nation.
So we have come to cash this check,
a check that will give us upon demand the riches of freedom
and the security of justice. ‖‖

We have also come to this hallowed spot
to remind America of the fierce urgency of now.
This is no time
[to engage in the luxury of cooling off or to take
the tranquilizing drug of gradualism. |

Now is the time
to make real the promises of democracy.
Now is the time
to rise from the dark and desolate valley of segregation to the sunlit path
of racial justice.
Now is the time
to lift our nation from the quicksands of racial injustice to the solid rock
of brotherhood.
Now is the time
to make justice a reality for all of God's children.

But there is something that I must say to my people
who stand on the warm threshold which leads into the palace of justice.
In the process of gaining our rightful place
we must not be guilty of wrongful deeds.
Let us not seek to satisfy our thirst for freedom
by drinking from the cup of bitterness and hatred.
We must forever conduct our struggle on the high plane of dignity and discipline.
We must not allow our creative protest
to degenerate into physical violence.
Again and again
we must rise to the majestic heights
of meeting physical force with soul force.

5:30   6:00   7:00   8:00   9:30

It would be fatal for the nation
to overlook the urgency of the moment.
This sweltering summer of the Negro's legitimate discontent
will not pass
until there is an invigorating autumn of freedom and equality.
Nineteen sixty-three is not an end, but a beginning.
Those who hope
that the Negro needed to blow off steam
and will now be content
will have a rude awakening if the nation returns to business as usual.
There will be neither rest nor tranquility in America
until the Negro is granted his citizenship rights.
The whirlwinds of revolt will continue to shake the foundations of our nation
until the bright day of justice emerges.

The marvelous new militancy
which has engulfed the Negro community
must not lead us to a distrust of all white people,
for many of our white brothers, as evidenced by their presence here today,
have come to realize that their destiny is tied up with our destiny.
They have come to realize that their freedom is inextricably bound
to our freedom.
We cannot walk alone.
And as we walk,
we must make the pledge that we shall always march ahead.
We cannot turn back.

There are those who are asking the devotees of civil rights,
"When will you be satisfied?"
We can never be satisfied as long as
the Negro is the victim of the unspeakable horrors
of police brutality. We can never be satisfied
as long as our bodies, heavy with the fatigue of travel,
cannot gain lodging in the motels of the highways and the hotels of the cities.
We cannot be satisfied
as long as the Negro's basic mobility is from a smaller ghetto to a larger one.
We can never be satisfied
as long as our children are stripped of their selfhood and robbed of their dignity by signs stating "For Whites Only."
We cannot be satisfied as long as a Negro
in Mississippi cannot vote
and a Negro in New York believes he has nothing for which to vote.

What could be

What is

No, we are not satisfied, and we will not be satisfied until "justice rolls down like waters, and righteousness like a mighty stream." |||

I am not unmindful
that some of you have come here
out of great trials and tribulations.
Some of you have come fresh from narrow jail cells.
Some of you have come from areas where your quest for freedom
left you battered by the storms of persecution
and staggered by the winds of police brutality.
You have been the veterans of creative suffering.
Continue to work with the faith
that unearned suffering
is redemptive.

10:00

Go back to Mississippi, go back to Alabama, go back to South Carolina, go back to Georgia, go back to Louisiana, go back to the slums and ghettos of our northern cities,
knowing that somehow this situation can and will be changed.
Let us not wallow in the valley of despair,
I say to you today, my friends, ||
so even though
we face the difficulties
of today and tomorrow,

I still have a dream.
It is a dream deeply rooted in the American dream.
I have a dream

11:00

that one day
this nation will rise up
and live out the true meaning of its creed:
"We hold these truths to be self-evident, that all men are created equal." ||

I have a dream

12:00

that one day on the red hills of Georgia
the sons of former slaves and the sons of former slave owners
will be able to sit down together at the table of brotherhood.

that one day

will be transformed into an oasis of freedom and justice.

I have a dream |

that my four little children
will one day live in a nation where they will not be judged by the color of their skin
but by the content of their character.

13:00

that one day,
down
in Alabama, with its vicious racists,
with its governor
having his lips dripping with the words of interposition and nullification;

I have a dream today. ||
I have a dream

I have a dream |

even the state of Mississippi, a state sweltering with the heat of injustice, sweltering with the heat of oppression,

I have a dream |

one day right there in Alabama, little black boys and black girls will be able to join hands with little white boys and white girls as sisters and brothers,

I have a dream today. ||
I have a dream

that one day every valley shall be exalted,
every hill and mountain shall be made low, the rough places will be made plain,
and the crooked places will be made straight,
and the glory of the Lord shall be revealed, and all flesh
shall see it together.
This is our hope.
This is the faith that I go back to the South with.
With this faith
we will be able to hew out of the mountain of despair a stone of hope.
With this faith
we will be able to transform the jangling discords of our nation
into a beautiful symphony of brotherhood.
With this faith
we will be able to work together, to pray together, to struggle together,
to go to jail together,
to stand up for freedom together, knowing
that we will be free one day. |
And this will be the day;
this will be the day when all of God's children
will be able to sing with new meaning,
"My country, 'tis of thee,
sweet land of liberty, of thee I sing.
Land where my fathers died, land of the pilgrim's pride,
from every mountainside,
let freedom ring." And if America is to be a great nation
this must become true.
So let freedom ring
from the prodigious hilltops of New Hampshire.
Let freedom ring
from the mighty mountains of New York.
Let freedom ring
from the heightening Alleghenies of Pennsylvania!
Let freedom ring
from the snowcapped Rockies of Colorado!
Let freedom ring
from the curvaceous slopes of California!
But not only that;
let freedom ring from Stone Mountain of Georgia! |
Let freedom ring from Lookout Mountain of Tennessee! |
Let freedom ring from every hill and molehill of Mississippi.
From every mountainside,
let freedom ring. And when this happens, ||
when we allow freedom ring,
when we let it ring from every village and every hamlet,
from every state
and every city,
we will be able to speed up that day when all of God's children, black men]
and white men,
Jews and Gentiles, Protestants and Catholics,
will be able to join hands and sing in the words of the old Negro spiritual,
"Free at last! free a last!
thank God Almighty,
we are free at last!' |||

1:00
5:00
16:00
16:30

Speaking
Repetition
Metaphor, Visual Words
Familiar Songs, Scripture, Literature
Political Reference
| Applause
|| Heavy Applause
||| Sustained Applause and Cheering
[ ] No pause at end of line break

Case Study: Martha Graham
Showed the World How She Felt

Although primarily known as a dancer, Martha Graham was also a powerful communicator. She developed characteristics that anyone who aspires to become a great presenter must cultivate and nourish. She stood out by moving against the grain of society. She persevered in spite of seemingly overwhelming obstacles. She fought against and overcame her fears. She respected and connected deeply with her audience. And she never held back from communicating her deepest feelings.

Graham spent her life challenging what dance is and what a dancer can do. She looked upon dance as an exploration, a celebration of life, and a religious calling that required absolute devotion.[13]

Graham became a dancer against the odds. She grew up in an environment where dance was frowned upon as a career. **When she finally began to study dance with the idea of making it her profession, she was considered too old, too short, too heavy, and too homely to be taken seriously.** "They thought I was good enough to be a teacher, but not a dancer," she recalled. But she knew what she wanted to do and pursued her goal with the intensity that marked her entire life. Dance was her reason for living. Willing to risk everything, driven by a burning passion, she dedicated herself absolutely to her art. "I did not choose to be a dancer," she often said. "I was chosen."[14]

To Graham, traditional European ballet seemed decadent and undemocratic. Classical ballet dated back more than three hundred years, when it originated as an elegant spectacle in the royal courts of Europe. Ballet was a highly controlled dance form, characterized by grace and precision of movement—but not freedom of expression.

Graham was ready to discard traditional ballet. She invented a revolutionary new language of dance, an original way of moving with which she revealed the joys, passions, and sorrows common to human experience. In place of graceful soaring leaps through space, she introduced stark, angular movements, blunt gestures, and stern facial expressions as she sought to lay bare fundamental human moods and feelings. Her dances were meant to be challenging and disturbing.[15]

This new kind of dance wasn't to everyone's liking, as it was neither beautiful nor romantic. Graham was often the object of ridicule and the butt of hostile jokes. Women in America had won the right to vote only a few years earlier, in 1920, and many people were still uncomfortable with the image of the "new woman" who sought a career and voted. It was acceptable to be a high-kicking, scantily clad chorus girl, but a woman who ran a dance company and created works that commented on war, poverty, and intolerance seemed unnatural and suspicious.[16]

She was protesting. Stark. And American. Some called her ugly, others called her revolutionary. But Graham was resolute in her desire to communicate how she felt.

"There is a vitality, a life force, an energy, a quickening that is translated through you into action, and because there is only one of you in all of time, this expression is unique. And if you block it, it will never exist through any other medium and it will be lost."

Martha Graham

Martha Graham
Dancer, Martha Graham Company

Graham believed that the secret, emotional world made visible by a dancer's movement could not always be expressed in words. She wanted her dances to be "felt" rather than "understood."[17] Graham drew inspiration from the ugly side of life and put it on display. Each of her dances had a special significance to her, because they expressed a fear she had conquered in her own life.

In 1930, Graham premiered a haunting solo dance of mourning called *Lamentation.* www These rare photos show her sitting on a low bench, wearing a tubelike shroud with only her face, hands, and bare feet showing. In the dance, she began to rock with anguish from side to side, plunging her hands deep into the stretchy fabric, writhing and twisting as if trying to break out of her own skin. She was a figure of unbearable sorrow and grief. She did not dance about grief but sought to be the *very embodiment* of grief.

Graham recalled, "One of the first times I performed it was in Brooklyn. A lady came back to me afterwards and looked at me. She was very white-faced and she'd obviously been crying. She said 'you'll never know what you have done for me tonight, thank you' and left. I asked about her later and it seemed that she had seen her nine-year-old son killed in front of her by a truck. She had made every effort to cry, but was unable to. But when she saw *Lamentation* she said she felt that grief was honorable and universal and that she should not be ashamed of crying for her son. I remember that story as a deep story in my life that made me realize that there is always one person to whom you speak in the audience. One."[18]

Graham moved in a way that gave anger and grief back to her audiences. **She had a genius for connecting movement with emotion. She could make visible all those feelings that people have inside them but can't put to words.**

Communicating in any medium is hard work. Graham's dances did not come easily to her. When the idea for a new dance was starting to take form, it was "a time of great misery." Graham worked late into the night, propped up in bed, writing down thoughts, observations, impressions, quotations from books—anything that could help feed her imagination. "I would put a typewriter on a little table on my bed, bolster myself with pillows, and write all night."[19]

She read widely as she searched for ideas and inspiration, studying psychology, yoga, poetry, Greek myths, and the Bible. Gradually, the ideas that filled her notebooks would begin to reveal a pattern, and she would write out a detailed script.[20]

In her work, Graham repeatedly portrayed a woman called to a high destiny and forced to overcome fear before she could answer the call. This was personal, as Graham herself believed that she had been given "lonely, terrifying gifts"—a sort of divine command to penetrate the interior of the human spirit, no matter what comfortless truths she might find there.[21]

In 1955, the U.S. government asked Graham to tour major cities in seven countries as a cultural ambassador. She gave lectures at each stop but was a very nervous presenter. In the biography, *Martha,* author Agnes de Mille describes the scene. "She hung onto the barre, clung to the walls. She couldn't think what to do with her hands, with her robes, with her feet." Finally, she escaped into her dressing room and locked the door.[22] But Graham tried again and again, and she overcame her fear. Eventually, the State Department officials named Graham "the greatest single ambassador we have ever sent to Asia."[23]

Until she was ninety, Graham continued to deliver lectures, which she had developed into an art form. A striking figure with a seductive voice, poetic insights, and a faultless sense of timing, she learned how to hold an audience spellbound.[24]

You could say that by trying to discover herself, she founded the world of modern dance. During her long journey, she invented a new way of moving, a unique dance language that has thrilled audiences all over the world and enlarged our understanding of what it means to be human.[25]

All of us are unique. We each have our own pattern of creativity, and if we do not express it, it is lost for all time. Graham defied customs, broke through barriers, and presented new ideas. She was loved and reviled, yet persistent in overcoming her fears to communicate what she felt in her soul. By remaining committed to communicating how she felt, she changed dance for all time.

Be Transparent So People See Your Idea

You must be willing to be you, to be real, and to humbly expose your own heart if you want the people in the audience to open theirs. You must be transparent, and this is difficult. Standing in front of an audience is already a challenge in itself. When stage fright is compounded with the new demand on leaders to be transparent, it's downright terrifying.

Being transparent moves your natural tendency of personal promotion out of the way so there's more room for your idea to be noticed. The audience can see past you and see the idea.

There are three keys to being transparent:

- **Be honest:** Be honest with the audience and give them the authentic you. You're not perfect; they understand that. If you are honest with yourself and with them, your presentations will have more moments of vulnerability and sincerity. It's not honest to present yourself as the almighty-powerful-know-it-all-who-has-no-flaws. If you're genuine, your humanness will come through. This means sharing stories that open your listeners' hearts, sharing how you've failed and how you've overcome, and letting people in to see that you're real. Openly sharing moments of pain or pleasure endears you to the audience through transparency.

"Being true to yourself involves showing and sharing emotion. The spirit that motivates most great storytellers is 'I want you to feel what I feel,' and the effective narrative is designed to make this happen. That's how the information is bound to the experience and rendered unforgettable."

Peter Guber[26]

- **Be unique:** No two people have experienced the exact same trials and triumphs in life. During your lifetime, you've collected stories and feelings that no one else has. It's those differences that make you interesting. Though we often tend to conceal our differences in an effort to fit in and be accepted, our unique perspective is what brings new insights to a topic. Share your ideas and be okay with the fact that sometimes you're the only one who sees what you see.

- **Don't compromise:** If you really believe in what you're communicating, speak confidently about it and don't back down. It's scary to be ridiculed or rejected, but sometimes that's the price. It won't be easy to try something no one has done before or speak loudly about a topic that no one has the guts to confront. Be encouraged by the child in the story of "The Emperor's New Clothes" who had the guts to say what was really going on and, in doing so, shattered the pretenses of the entire royal court. Call it like it is.

I want to be
transparent so
they can see what
I'm saying. To decrease
the focus on me so my
idea will be seen. Ideas
either die or get adopted
based on how they are
conveyed. If I am honest,
they will feel what I feel.
Being real and humble
will help amplify what
I'm trying to say.
I refuse to give up
because I really
believe this is
the right thing
to do. It feels
like I'm the
only one who sees
what needs to happen,
so I will do whatever it takes
to get my idea into the hearts

You Can Transform Your World

Whether your opportunity to convey your passion comes through work or other activities, there will be a moment in your life when making an idea clear will play a significant role in shaping who you become—and the legacy you leave behind.

Your ideas may be simple, or they could contain the keys that unlock unknown mysteries. However, if you don't communicate them well, they will lose their value and add nothing to humanity.

The amount of value you place on your idea should be reflected in the amount of care you take in communicating it. **Passion for your idea should drive you to invest in its communication.**

In this book, we've looked at several people whose presentations changed the status quo. Their communications graced the world and made it a better place. These presenters came from different faiths, different walks of life, and different passions; yet all of them made the personal investment required to communicate effectively and change their world. When looking at the profound impact they've all had, it's easy to tell yourself that you won't measure up to their standards because presenting came naturally to them and doesn't come naturally to you. That's simply not true.

The people featured in this book invested many hours in their presentations and agonized over the words, structure, and delivery of their ideas. Their presentations didn't come easily to them, but they were all committed to conveying their perspective in a way that was successfully persuasive. Some even risked their lives for their ideas.

If you aren't inspired by what you do—or if you don't have a message to convey that you're passionate about—find your calling. This book looked at a motivator, a marketer, a politician, a conductor, a lecturer, a preacher, an executive, an activist, and an artist. They all had their own well of inspirational ideas and their own unique way of communicating them. You can too. You just need to find what inspires passion in you. Then you must apply the same discipline to communicating it as musicians or dancers apply to their craft.

Nowadays, more than any other time, people are eager for inspired ideas that stand out and are worth believing in. There's so much disingenuous noise in our culture that when an idea is presented with sincerity and passion, it stands out and resonates.

We were born to create ideas; getting people to feel like they have a stake in what we believe is the hard part.

It doesn't seem fair that an idea's worth is judged by how well it's presented, but it happens every day. **So, if you can communicate an idea well, you have, within you, the power to change the world.**

GO
CHANGE
YOUR
WORLD

Inspiration Is Everywhere

Case Study: Wolfgang Amadeus Mozart
Be Flexible Within the Form

Classical music includes a structure called the sonata form, which is similar to the presentation form. A sonata has standard "rules" to follow, yet each sonata sounds unique. Sonatas don't come across as contrived or formulaic, and we can draw inspiration for our presentations from that.

Structure in the Three-Part Sonata Form
Structure enables listeners to anticipate what comes next. The sonata form has three parts:

1 Beginning (exposition): Musical themes are introduced and usually repeated so the listener can identify the central musical idea. It's important that the listeners thoroughly understand the initial theme, so they can recognize it when it's modified (creating an identifiable gap between *what is* and *what could be*).

2 Middle (development): The musical theme is altered and riffed off of. This is the most exciting part of the piece, because the listeners are intrigued by how the composer modifies the central idea. The listeners can hear the tension between what the theme was in the beginning and what it has become during the development. There is an element of surprise.

3 End (recapitulation): After the ideas are modified in the development section, the piece transitions back to the original theme. There is a special feeling when that theme is restated after its modification during the development section.

Contrast Keeps Things Interesting
Contrast keeps a presentation interesting. The same is true with music.

4 Tonal contrast: Put simply, tonal contrast is key changes. Ben Zander mentions in his presentation (page 48) that music has a "home" or place of resolution for which it longs. That home is the tonic key. The beauty of harmony is that the human ear recognizes when we are away from home and when we are home.

5 Dynamic contrast: Dynamic contrast is created when the music alternates between loud and soft. Sometimes the transition is sudden, while other times it is gradual.

6 Textural contrast:
a. Polyphony/Monophony—Throughout the piece there is always a clear melodic line. Sometimes all the instruments play the same melody in unison (monophony), and other times one instrument plays the melody while the others complement and accompany the melody (polyphony).
b. Density—The number of notes played per measure determines the density. Sometimes there are only a few notes per measure, while at other times there are many, often being played at the same time.

The foundation for an interesting sonata is that it has contrast in varying layers, similar to a presentation. Just like a great sonata, a great presentation should follow the structure of the presentation form yet be flexible within its constraint. As the composer of your presentation, you need to create dramatic contrast to keep the audience's interest piqued.

Sonata Form[1]

EXPOSITION			DEVELOPMENT	RECAPITULATION		
	A	:	B		A	
a	b	c	a b c	a	b	c
Tonic	Dominant	Dominant	Foreign Keys	Tonic	Tonic	Tonic

Each of the numbered items in blue circles above is represented in the sparkline on the following pages.

Wolfgang Amadeus Mozart
Austrian Composer

Sonata Sparkline

Below is my son's analysis of the structure and contrast in the first movement of Mozart's *Eine kleine Nachtmusik*. You can see the clear structure of the beginning (1), development/middle (2), and recapitulation/end (3). The most important contrast in music is the tonal contrast (4). Also notice how extensive the other two forms of contrast are, (5) and (6). Contrast is important.

No two sonatas are alike because great composers know how to work flexibly within the form. For your inspiration, there are sonatas visualized and set to music on this book's web site. www

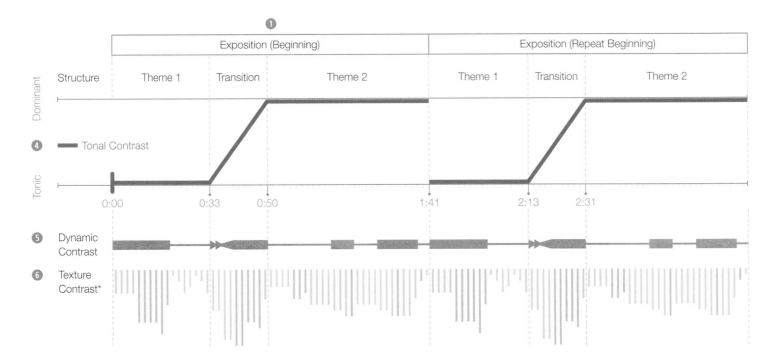

*Texture contrast is represented by *color* and *bar height.* Yellow represents musicians playing in unison, blue represents each playing something different, and green is a blend of the two. The height of the bars represents the density of the music. Short bars represent fewer notes per measure (typical of slow music), and longer bars represent more notes per measure (typical of fast music).

A *coda* is additional material that's played after the reca-pitulation has ended. Steve Jobs's presentations often have "codas." Just when you think he's unveiled everything, he has an "Oh, wait! There's more!" moment.

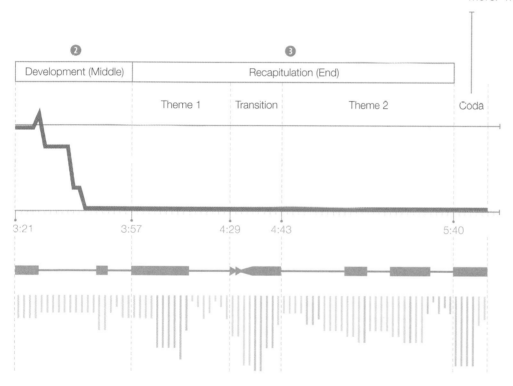

❷ Development (Middle)

❸ Recapitulation (End)

Theme 1   Transition   Theme 2   Coda

3:21   3:57   4:29   4:43   5:40

Case Study: Alfred Hitchcock
Be a Collaborative Visionary

The presenter is the public persona of a single individual, but in reality, the best presentations result from the collaborative efforts of an empowered team behind the scenes.

Alfred Hitchcock controlled the central creative aspects of his films, but he relied heavily on his team in their creative development and production. Ideas were *written* and *drawn* before they were filmed. **Hitchcock worked with a screenwriter to develop a written framework (the script). He then worked with a production designer to create a visual framework (sketches and storyboards).**[2]

- **Written Framework:** To Hitchcock, the real creative work on a film took place in the office of the writer. "We went into a huddle and slowly from discussions, arguments, random suggestions, casual desultory talk, and furious intellectual quarrels as to what such and such a character in such and such a situation would or would not do, the scenario began to take shape."[3]

  Without a doubt, Hitchcock brought out the very best in his writers. They created absorbing stories, developed interesting characters, and provided compelling dialogue. Combined with Hitchcock's direction, the result was a body of work unmatched in the cinema.[4]

- **Visual Framework:** Hitchcock constantly visualized his movies. He began with a story or idea and moved quickly to develop a look for the film. Each step in the process—costume design, production design, set design, visual effects, written scene descriptions, shot lists, storyboards, and camera angle drawings—included a conversation with the appropriate department heads. Hitchcock's collaborators usually took one of the director's suggestions and expanded upon it, integrating their ideas into the collective process. Hitchcock envisioned

his films in detail before the camera began to roll.[5] When interviewed by French film director Francois Truffaut in 1962, Hitchcock boasted, "I never look at a script while I'm shooting. I know the whole film by heart."[6]

Actress Janet Leigh described his modus operandi: "In his mind, and sketched on the pages of his script, the film was already shot. He showed me the model sets and moved the miniature camera through the tiny furniture toward the wee dolls, exactly the way he intended to do in the "reel" life. Meticulously thorough down to the minutest detail."[7]

The process of creating a movie is a highly collaborative one in which each person involved brings a layer of value. The better we understand the creative process behind motion pictures, the better we can understand the creative process behind an effective presentation.

Great leaders honor the people behind the curtain that help with their presence on stage. Leading requires that you bring out the best in the team supporting you. Use their strengths and talents to build on your ideas. Be open to modifying your vision by embracing the unique value they bring to the project.

Even though Hitchcock was the one in the spotlight, he let many others influence his work.

My dad, to whom this book is dedicated, was a contributor to *Alfred Hitchcock's Mystery Magazine*. I've posted his short stories online. www

On each film, Hitchcock meticulously planned out shots, camera movement, and even details like the number of birds in the shot and the distance of the camera from the action. Then, a storyboard artist sketched his vision.[8]

Alfred Hitchcock
English Filmmaker and Producer

Case Study: E. E. Cummings
Break the Rules

E. E. Cummings was an American poet, painter, essayist, author, and playwright. He graduated from Harvard magna cum laude and then continued (still at Harvard) to get a Master's degree in English and Classical Studies. He loved writing, so to become a better writer, he signed up for an advanced composition class where his teacher taught him how to make his writing clearer, more precise, and less wordy. Cummings practiced writing until his wrist hurt.[9] Even though he was considered an avant-garde poet, much of his work falls within traditional poetic forms. For example, many of his poems are sonnets (but with a modern twist), and he occasionally made use of the blues form and acrostic poems.

Cummings knew the *right* way to write. He didn't break the rules until he fully understood them. Cummings continually asked himself, "What else can language be made to do?"[10]

He combined his love for poetry and art by using the text itself as a form. He tore words apart as a way of separating letters and the sounds of syllables from their meaning. He also stretched out words and used punctuation marks and capital letters to add meaning or create visual and aural effects. He forced readers to read slowly, to relish sounds as they gradually put the words back together and discovered what the poems truly meant.[11]

The public did not initially enjoy his work—he broke too many rules, and his ideas were too far out for the general public to consume. For decades, he was reviled by the poetry community, and he struggled to make ends meet. As he eagerly submitted poetry to publishers, one after another told him, "No thanks." After fourteen publishers turned down his book, he printed it himself. He called it *No Thanks,* and in it he printed the names of the fourteen publishers who had rejected him in a list shaped like a funeral urn.[12]

It wasn't until he was fifty-six years old that his poetry began to get the recognition that it deserved. As his career picked up momentum, he traveled and conducted readings of his poems to packed auditoriums, becoming the best-known poet in the United States. No American poet has ever been more playful than Cummings, and none have been more skillful at arranging words on a page. Many poets have imitated his style, but their attempts only prove how difficult it is to master that style.[13] He was a true revolutionary.

It's important to know the rules so you understand how to flex and even break them to create meaning.

Many of the people who changed the world broke the rules and went against standard convention. They stood out, were different, and were even reviled at times. Sometimes an idea stands out so much it shocks people, but that's what it takes to be noticed. Your idea might initially be rejected—but take heart—persistence will move it from rejected to considered and eventually adopted. Communicate it until you know you've done everything in your power to help your heroes on their journey.

f

  eeble a blu
r of cr
umbli
ng m

oo

  n(
poor shadoweaten
was
of is and un of

so

)h
    ang
    s
    from

thea lmo st mor ning[14]

Sometimes Cummings pried a word open with a phrase wrapped in parentheses to show that two events or thoughts were occurring at the same time.[15]

During World War II, the U.S. government rounded up Japanese Americans on the West Coast—many of them U.S. citizens—and forced them to live in prison camps. Cummings's outrage found expression in poetry that mimics intolerance based on ignorance.[16]

ygUDuh

    ydoan
    yunnuhstan

    ydoan o
    yunnuhstan dem
    yguduh ged

    yunnuhstan dem doidee
    yguduh ged riduh
    ydoan o nudn
LISN bud LISN

      dem
      gud
      am

      lidl yelluh bas
      tuds weer goin

duhSIVILEYEzum[17]

(If the meaning is unclear, try reading the lines aloud.)

if there are any heavens my mother will(all by herself)have
one. It will not be a pansy heaven nor
a fragile heaven of lilies-of-the-valley but
it will be a heaven of blackred roses

my father will be(deep like a rose
tall like a rose)

standing near my

(swaying over her
silent)
with eyes which are really petals and see

nothing with the face of a poet really which
is a flower and not a face with
hands
which whisper
This is my beloved my

            (suddenly in sunlight
he will bow,

& the whole garden will bow)[18]

Cummings imagines his
mother and father in
Heaven. He leaves some
words unwritten, reminding
us of the way speech can
trail off into thought and
how words unspoken can
still be understood.[19]

Your ideas are potent. A single idea from the human mind can change the world. Mozart, Hitchcock, and Cummings all revolutionized their fields by exploring and developing new ideas that had never existed.

You have the opportunity to shape the future through your imagination. Imagining a future where your idea has been implemented will keep you inspired to communicate your idea passionately.

So be flexible, be visionary, and now go rewrite all the rules.

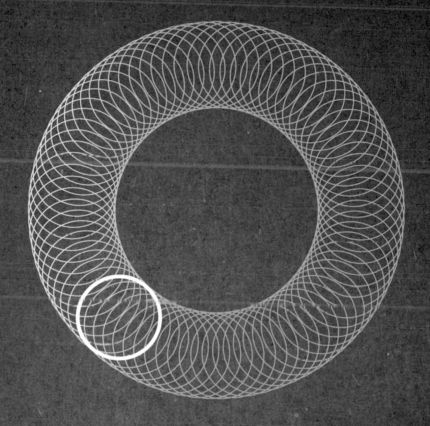

RULE #9

Your imagination
can create a reality.

James Cameron

References

CHAPTER 1

1. Guber, Peter. "The Four Truths of the Storyteller." *Harvard Business Review.* December 1, 2007.

2. Godin, Seth. "Too Much Data Leads to Not Enough Belief." From Seth Godin's Blog. January 21, 2010. http://sethgodin.typepad.com/seths_blog/2010/01/too-much-data-leads-to-not-enough-belief.html.

3. Aristotle. *The Art of Rhetoric.* London: Penguin Books, 1991.

4. Guy De Maupassant, Henri René Albert. *The Works of Guy de Maupassant: Volume VIII.* New York: Bigelow, Smith, and Co, 1909.

5. Sturm, Brian W. "The 'Storylistening' Trance Experience." *Journal of American Folklore.* 113, 2000.

6. McKee, Robert. "Storytelling That Moves People." *Harvard Business Review.* June 1, 2003.

7. Chad Hodge as quoted in: Guber, Peter. "The Four Truths of the Storyteller." *Harvard Business Review.* December 1, 2007.

CHAPTER 2

1. Hart, Jack. *A Writer's Coach: The Complete Guide to Writing Strategies That Work.* New York: Anchor Books, 2006.

2. Reynolds, Garr. *Presentation Zen: Simple Ideas on Presentation Design and Delivery.* Berkeley: New Riders, 2008.

3. McKee, Robert. *Story: Substance, Structure, Style, and The Principles of Screenwriting.* New York: ReganBooks, 1997.

4. Field, Syd. *Screenplay: The Foundations of Screenwriting.* New York: Delta, 2005.

5. © Syd Field 1980, 2000.

6. Vogler, Chris. *The Writer's Journey: Mythic Structure for Writers, 3rd Edition.* Studio City: Michael Wiese Productions, 2007.

7. Campbell, Joseph. *The Hero with a Thousand Faces.* Novato: New World Library, 2008.

8. Euripides. *Aegeus.*

9. McKee, Robert. *Story: Substance, Structure, Style, and The Principles of Screenwriting.* New York: ReganBooks, 1997.

10. Hazlitt, William. *Selected Writings.* Oxford: Oxford University Press, 1991.

11. Vogler, Chris. *The Writer's Journey: Mythic Structure for Writers, 3rd Edition.* Studio City: Michael Wiese Productions, 2007.

12. Guber, Peter. "The Four Truths of the Storyteller." *Harvard Business Review.* December 1, 2007.

13. Eliot, T. S. "Little Gidding." *Four Quartets.* San Diego: Harcourt, Inc., 1943.

CHAPTER 3

1. Ken Haemer as quoted in: Zelazny, Gene. *Say It with Presentations: How to Design and Deliver Successful Business Presentations.* New York: McGraw-Hill, 2006.

2. Broad, William J. "The Shuttle Explodes." *New York Times.* January 29, 1986.

3. 4. 5. Eidenmuller, Michael E. *Great Speeches for Better Speaking.* New York: McGraw-Hill, 2008. 31–37.

6. Snyder, Blake. *Save the Cat! The Last Book on Screenwriting You'll Ever Need.* Studio City: Michael Weise Productions, 2005.

7. Defoe, Daniel. *The Complete English Tradesman.* London: Biblio Bazaar, 2006.

CHAPTER 4

1. James, Geoffrey. "Create a Dynamite Presentation in 6 Easy Steps." *Sales Machine.* BNET article. http://blogs.bnet.com/salesmachine/?p=9603.

2. Kotter, John P. "Leading Change: Why Transformation Efforts Fail." *Harvard Business Review.* January 1, 2007.

3. Snyder, Blake. *Save the Cat! The Last Book on Screenwriting You'll Ever Need.* Studio City: Michael Weise Productions, 2005.

4. Kotter, John P. and Leonard A. Shlesinger. "Choosing Strategies for Change. *Harvard Business Review.* July–August 2008.

CHAPTER 5

1. Aristotle. *The Art of Rhetoric.* London: Penguin Books, 1991.

2. Pascal, Blaise. *Pensées.* London: Penguin Books, 1995.

3. Olson, Randy. *Don't Be Such A Scientist.* Washington, D.C.: Island Press, 2009.

4. Martin, Roger. *The Design of Business: Why Design Thinking the Next Competitive Advantage.* Boston: Harvard Business Press, 2009.

5. Boettinger, Henry M. *Moving Mountains: The Art of Letting Others See Things Your Way.* New York: Macmillan Publishing Company, 1969.

6. Heritage, John and David Greatbatch, "Generating Applause: A Study of Rhetoric and Response at Party Political Conferences." *American Journal of Sociology.* 1986.

7. Gargiulo, Terrence. *Stories at Work.* Portsmouth: Greenwood Publishing Group, 2006.

8. McKee, Robert. *Story: Substance, Structure, Style, and The Principles of Screenwriting.* New York: ReganBooks, 1997.

9. 10. 11. Hughes, Glenn. Storytelling Template © HuesWorks.com.

12. Few, Stephen. *Now You See It.* Oakland: Analytics Press, 2009.

13. 14. Brown, Tim. *Change By Design.* New York: Harper Business, 2009.

15. Quiller-Couch, Sir Arthur. *On the Art of Writing.* Cambridge: Cambridge University Press, 1916.

CHAPTER 6

1. Boettinger, Henry M. *Moving Mountains: The Art of Letting Others See Things Your Way.* New York: Macmillan Publishing Company, 1969.

2. "The Pleasure of Finding Things Out." Horizon BBC Interview, 1983.

3. 4. 5. Feynman, Richard. *Classic Feynman: All the Adventures of a Curious Character.* New York: WW Norton and Company, 2006.

6. Bligh, Donald A. *What's the Use of Lectures?* San Francisco: Jossey-Bass Publishers, 2000.

7. Guber, Peter. "The Four Truths of the Storyteller." *Harvard Business Review.* December 1, 2007.

8. McKee, Robert. *Story: Substance, Structure, Style, and The Principles of Screenwriting.* New York: ReganBooks, 1997.

9. Duarte, Nancy. *Slide:ology: The Art and Science of Creating Great Presentations.* Sebastopol: O'Reilly, 2008.

CHAPTER 7

1. Feynman, Richard. *Classic Feynman: All the Adventures of a Curious Character.* New York: WW Norton and Company, 2006.

2. TED.com. http://www.ted.com/talks/lang/eng/bill_gates_unplugged.html.

3. Gallo, Carmine. *The Presentation Secrets of Steve Jobs.* New York: McGraw-Hill, 2010.

4. Carreau, Mark. "One Small Step for Clarity." *Houston Chronicle.* October 3, 2006. http://www.chron.com/disp/story.mpl/front/4225856.html.

5. "The Long Island Index's Scary Movie." *Newsday.* January 24, 2010.

6. Gallo, Carmine. *The Presentation Secrets of Steve Jobs.* New York: McGraw-Hill, 2010.

7. Evangelist, Mike. "Behind the Magic Curtain." *Guardian.* January 5, 2006. http://www.guardian.co.uk/technology/2006/jan/05/newmedia.media1.

8. 9. Gallo, Carmine. *The Presentation Secrets of Steve Jobs.* New York: McGraw-Hill, 2010.

CHAPTER 8

1. Shannon, C. E. "A Mathematical Theory of Communication." *The Bell System Technical Journal,* Vol. 27, pp. 379–423, 623–656, July, October, 1948. (The Shannon-Weaver Model was slightly modified and retrofitted to fit presentation communications.)

2. Gallo, Carmine. *The Presentation Secrets of Steve Jobs.* New York: McGraw-Hill, 2010.

3. Olson, Randy. *Don't Be Such A Scientist.* Washington, D.C.: Island Press, 2009.

4. Dr. Rollin D. Hotchkiss as quoted in the introduction to: Keller, Evelyn Fox. *A Feeling for the Organism: Life and Work of Barbara McClintock.* New York: Henry Holt, 2003.

5. Everett, Edward. *Papers of Edward Everett: an inventory.* Harvard: Harvard University Press, 2008.

6. Mayer, Richard E. *Multimedia Learning.* Cambridge: Cambridge University Press, 2009.

7. McKee, Robert. *Story: Substance, Structure, Style, and The Principles of Screenwriting.* New York: ReganBooks, 1997.

8. Olson, Randy. *Don't Be Such A Scientist.* Washington, D.C.: Island Press, 2009.

9. *Omnibus: Leonard Bernstein.* Produced by Robert Saudek Associates. RSA Venture, 1990.

10. Haws, Barbara. *Leonard Bernstein: American Original.* New York: Collins, 2008.

11. Bernstein, Leonard. *Young People's Concerts DVD.* West Long Branch: Kultur.

12. 13. 15. 17. Haws, Barbara. *Leonard Bernstein: American Original.* New York: Collins, 2008.

14. 16. From an interview with Barbara Haws, NY Philharmonic Archivist conducted by Nancy Duarte, May 2010.

CHAPTER 9

1. Boettinger, Henry M. *Moving Mountains: The Art of Letting Others See Things Your Way.* New York: Macmillan Publishing Company, 1969.

2. NASA Janitor story is an urban legend of sorts.

3. Hugo, Victor. *The History of a Crime.* Boston: Little, Brown and Company, 1909.

4. Neumeier, Marty. *The Designful Company: How to build a culture of nonstop innovation.* Berkeley: New Riders, 2009.

5. http://www.justice.gov/.

6. *USA Today.* September 15, 2002.

7. Boje, David and Grace Ann Rosile. "Enron Spectacles: A Critical Dramaturgical Analysis." *Organization Studies.* Vol. 25, No. 5, 751–774. New Mexico State University, 2004.

8. Banerjee, Neela. "At Enron, Lavish Excess Often Came Before Success." *New York Times.* February 26, 2002.

9. 10. 12. http://www.justice.gov/

10. 11. Behr, Peter and April Witt. "The Fall of Enron Series." *Washington Post.* August 1, 2002.

13. 14. 15. 16. 17. 19. 20. 23. 24. 25. Freedman, Russell. *Martha Graham: A Dancer's Life.* New York: Clarion Books, 1998.

18. YouTube video transcription. http://www.youtube.com/watch?v=Pb4-kpClZns.

21. 22. Acocella, Joan. "Martha Graham on Film." From: *Martha Graham Dance on Film DVD.* Criterion Collection, 2007.

26. Guber, Peter. "The Four Truths of the Storyteller." *Harvard Business Review.* December 1, 2007.

CODA

1. Copeland, Aaron. *What to Listen for in Music.* New York: Signet Classic, 1985.

2. 5. 6. 8. *Casting a Shadow.* Eds. Will Schmenner and Corinne Granof. Evanston: Northwestern University Press, 2007.

3. Hitchcock, Alfred. *Hitchcock on Hitchcock.* Ed. Sidney Gottlieb. Berkeley: University of California Press, 1995.

4. 7. Mogg, Ken. *The Alfred Hitchcock Story.* London: Titan Books, 1999.

9. 10. 11. 12. 13. 15. 16. 19. Reef, Catherine. *E.E. Cummings: A Poet's Life.* New York, Clarion Books, 2006.

14. "f/eeble a blu." Copyright © 1958, 1986, 1991 by the Trustees for the E. E. Cummings Trust.

17. "ygUDuh." Copyright 1944, © 1972, 1991 by the Trustees for the E. E. Cummings Trust.

18. "l(a." Copyright © 1958, 1986, 1991 by the Trustees for the E. E. Cummings Trust, from COMPLETE POEMS: 1904–1962 by E. E. Cummings, edited by George J. Firmage. Used by permission of Liveright Publishing Corporation.

Picture Credits

PERSUASION IS POWERFUL 2, 3
Benjamin Zander: TED/Andrew Heavens, Beth Comstock: Photographed by Frank Mari, Ronald Reagan: Courtesy Ronald Reagan Library, Leonard Bernstein: AP Photo/Terhune, Richard Feynman: Courtesy of the Archives, California Institute of Technology, Pastor John Ortberg: Courtesy of Menlo Park Presbyterian Church, Steve Jobs: AP Photo/Paul Sakuma, Martin Luther King Jr.: AFP/Getty Images, © Barbara Morgan/Courtesy of the Martha Graham Center of Contemporary Dance

RESONANCE CAUSES CHANGE 5
Chladni plates: Photographed by Anthony Duarte

PRESENTATIONS ARE BORING 9
Hand: ©iStockphoto.com/Владислав Сусой

THE BLAND LEADING THE BLAND 11
Camouflage Man: Symphonie/Getty Images

PEOPLE ARE INTERESTING 13
Guy behind board: Photographed by Mark Heaps

Cork board: ©iStockphoto.com/Maxim Sergienko

STORIES CONVEY MEANING 17
Projector screen: ©iStockphoto.com/Nancy Louie

YOU ARE NOT THE HERO 18
All-about-me guy (Ryan Orcutt): Photographed by Mark Heaps

THE AUDIENCE IS THE HERO 21
Luke Skywalker & Yoda: Courtesy of Lucasfilm Ltd, *Star Wars: Episode V – The Empire Strikes Back* TM & © 1980 and 1997 Lucasfilm Ltd. All rights reserved. Used under authorization. Unauthorized duplication is a violation of applicable law.

THE MIDDLE: CONTRAST 41
M.C. Escher: M.C. Escher's "Circle Limit IV" © 2009 The M.C. Escher Company-Holland. All rights reserved. www.mcescher.com

CASE STUDY: BENJAMIN ZANDER 49
Ben Zander: TED/Andrew Heavens

HOW DO YOU RESONATE WITH THESE FOLKS? 57
Duarte Heroes: Photographed by Mark Heaps

SEGMENT THE AUDIENCE 59
Beers: ©iStockphoto.com/Julián Rovagnati

CASE STUDY: RONALD REAGAN 61
Ronald Reagan: Courtesy Ronald Reagan Library

ACKNOWLEDGE THE RISK 84
Butterflies: ©iStockphoto.com/Jordan McCullough

CASE STUDY: GENERAL ELECTRIC 90
Beth Comstock: Photographed by Dave Russell

EVERYTHING AND THE KITCHEN SINK 99
Stack of sticky notes: ©iStockphoto.com/Marek Uliasz

DON'T BE SO CEREBRAL 102
Arnold Schwarzenegger: ©Mirkine/Sygma/Corbis

TRANSFORM IDEAS INTO MEANING 100, 107
Nancy's Gram: Photographed by Barbara Childs

Nancy's Gram's teacup: Photographed by Paula Tesch

RECALL STORIES 109
Nancy's sister, Norma

MOVE FROM DATA TO MEANING 116
Hans Rosling: TED/Robert Leslie

ESTABLISH STRUCTURE 127
Figures (James Wachira and Krystin Brazie) behind glass: Photographed by Mark Heaps

CASE STUDY: RICHARD FEYNMAN 131
Richard Feynman: Courtesy of the Archives, California Institute of Technology

CREATE A S.T.A.R. MOMENT 149
Richard Feynman: Diana Walker/TIME & LIFE Images/Getty Images

Bill Gates: TED/James Duncan Davidson

Steve Jobs: AP Photo/Paul Sakuma

CASE STUDY: MICHAEL POLLAN 150
Michael Pollan: flickr/Pete Foley

Index

Special Thanks

It takes a village to write a visual book. Special thanks to the following for their support:

Art Direction and Cover Design: Diandra Macias
Page Layout: Michaela Kastlova

Design Assistance: Ryan Orcutt, Erik Chappins, James Nepomuceno, Kristin Bialaszewski, Shirley Ng-Benitez, and Nichole Nye

Project Manager: Krystin Brazie

Development Editing: Eric Albertson and Michael Moon

Copy Editing: Mike Stevens and Krystin Brazie

Researchers: Barbara Childs, Shuquio Song, Jim Vogt, James Ford, Monica Bolger, Lisa Klein, Tracy Barba, Jeremy Wick, Trish Gilfoil, Lisa Gallo, Sunni Brown, and Bernhard Kast

Conceptual Feedback: Raymond Nasr, Glenn Hughes, Sheri Benjamin, James Buckhouse, W. Hugo Van Vuuren, Jan Shultink, Lisa Gallo, Alex Varanese, Ezra Barany, and Anthony Duarte

Photography: Mark Heaps, Paula Tesch, and Jordan Brazie
Photo Retouching: Mark Heaps
Resonance Rule Design: Ryan Orcutt

Image Sourcing: Krystin Brazie, Juli Walwyn, Tina Salvatore. Thanks to Barbara Haws and Richard Wandel of the New York Philharmonic archives, Marie Carter of the Leonard Bernstein Office, Suzy Upton of the Martha Graham Dance Center, Jason Wishnow and Laura Galloway of TED, The CalTech Archives, The Writer's House (MLK), and the United States Library of Congress.

Transcription: Kristin Zailer and Melissa Duarte

Proofing: Anthony Duarte, Marisa Serapio, and Jeff Pena

there.

When you are ready to move your audience from here to there, Duarte can help you simplify complex ideas, develop a story, and communicate in a strikingly visual way. Focused exclusively on presentations, we offer best-in-class content, design, training, and technology.

info@duarte.com | 650.964.6745 | www.duarte.com

 DUARTE

Come and get it.

Whether you need to close a deal, propel a social cause, or engage the troops, presentation literacy gives you competitive advantage. Workshops from Duarte Academy help you master our VisualStory™ methodology so that you can start activating audiences immediately.

training@duarte.com | 650.964.6745 | www.duarte.com

D | DUARTE

Presentation Map™

Audience Empathy Map™

Glance Test™

duarte.com

reson

work:boo

The Pocket Diagrammer™

slide:olog

THE ART AND SCIE
OF CREATING GRE
PRESENTATIONS